VICTORY!

VICTORY!

PROPAGANDA CARTOONS FROM WORLD WAR II

EDITED BY TONY HUSBAND

Picture research: Frances Evans

With thanks to Gerald Patejunas

This edition published in 2022 by Sirius Publishing, a division of
Arcturus Publishing Limited,
26/27 Bickels Yard, 151–153 Bermondsey Street,
London SE1 3HA

Design: Notion Design

ISBN: 978-1-3988-1779-1
AD002537UK

Printed in China

CONTENTS

INTRODUCTION

I try to imagine how it must have felt to be a cartoonist during World War II: walking to the office through the bombed streets of your city, diving for cover as the air raid sirens sounded all around you, worrying about friends and loved ones as you listened to daily news from the front.

Life must have been very up and down, with stories of the gains, stories of the losses, and, all the time, lists of the dead, the dying and the missing. You would have found yourself sitting in on the editor's conference, the latest headlines in place and only the matter of your cartoon to be resolved. You'd go to your desk to be faced with the usual blank page. What a responsibility. And what pressure there must have been. Your job was to portray the mood of a nation, to put down in drawn lines a nation's anger, fear and hope. At the back of your mind, you would know that the cartoon was what people would remember, not the headline, not the thousands of printed words, but the image.

Images define a war. They capture a moment in time and lodge it in the nation's memory. Your cartoon would have to resonate with the soldier, the sailor and the candlestick-maker as well as the airman at the front, the factory girl, the farmer and the retired banker on air raid duty.

What is so wonderful about the cartoons in this collection is how many cartoonists rose so brilliantly to the challenge. Their pens and minds were sharpened to a fine point by the responsibility put upon them by the gravity of the situation. They produced masterpieces on a daily basis. From every corner of the world, from every side of the conflict, cartoonists of every nation fired their savage, subtle barbs into the heart of the enemy. How Hitler and his henchmen must have raged at the images of them drawn

Left: 'The Baubles of a Prime Minister – When the war is over we can start the rebuilding process' by Erich Schilling, Josef Goebbels' favourite cartoonist, 1941

Opposite: Adolf Hitler by Kukryniksy, the collective name for three Russian caricaturists, Porfirii Krylov, Mikhail Kuprilianov and Nikolai Sokolov (see page 106), 1942

in foreign newspapers. Similarly, Churchill, chomping on his cigar and drinking his nightly whisky, would have sighed at the pompous, drunken fool they made out of him.

It must have been really exciting to be a cartoonist then. You were given absolute freedom to vent your rage, to provide a piece of your mind. There were practically no limits. You could characterize your enemy as graphically as you wanted. You could distort and defame anyone on the other side. Indeed it was your duty to do so.

What better way to gain revenge on the perpetrators of crimes than with your pen? I know this from personal experience; I was once beaten up by a gang of skinheads and have spent the last 30 years getting my revenge on them by drawing them as louts and buffoons in magazines and newspapers. To be able to magnify that 100 times during wartime must have been very satisfying indeed

All nations, all sides are represented in this book. It is amazing and fascinating to see how each side's artists handle the war: the British subtle, laid-

Roosevelt as seen by English cartoonist E.H. Shepard in 1940 when France had fallen and the US president had appealed to Congress for Allied supplies

THICKER THAN WATER

"Now, Sam, step on it!"

back… tea and crumpets with the vicar, discussing progress on all fronts. The Russians, savage, satirical… Hitler the demon, as demon he surely was. There was no holding the Russians back from a full frontal assault, the pen scratching venom deeper and deeper into the paper. Cartoonists from the USA showed the ups and downs of GI Joe in a foreign country missing home comforts, while the Germans spat vitriol at anyone who opposed their plan for world domination and made scapegoats of those they had chosen to victimize.

I wonder too who was the crazy Japanese cartoonist who took time before the bombing of Pearl Harbor to draw up a leaflet to drop on the Americans. Crudely duplicated in thousands, the cartoon survived for posterity, a treacherous act by an unknown artist, but did Americans laugh at the words on the picture as we do today?

I am awed at the quality and variety of work here. From mighty historical and beautifully crafted pieces of art to the few lines scribbled quickly on an A4 sheet of paper, they all tell the tale of a moment

IN FRONT OF THE CURTAIN

"Please keep your seats—there's no danger."

Stalin drawn by E.H. Shepard with more than a whiff of sulphur: the Werth Questionnaire was a series of questions submitted to Stalin in 1946 by Alexander Werth of the *Sunday Times*. Stalin used his responses to paint a rosy picture of the Soviet Union as a benevolent giant with the friendliest of intentions towards its neighbours

in history. You can see during the build-up to the war that cartoonists were warning of the grim nature of events to come, the stupidity of failing to learn from history and the shock felt in the aftermath. Simply and surely within these pages, the views from all sides unfold and you can see how very similar they often were, just told in a different way. In those far-off days, cartoonists had great power. They were the stars of their newspapers and had salaries to match their status. They were much sought after and closely guarded by proprietors who dreaded losing them to rivals. Sadly it isn't the same these days, apart from a cherished few. Cartoonists used to be very influential and much feared. As a cartoonist I envy them that. They used that power to great purpose and left us with towering, unforgettable images. If I had a hat, I'd take it off to them. Enjoy the work within these pages. It is very special.

Tony Husband

AMERICAN RELI
LIST OF HOSTAGES SHOT

'Goering's Banquet': the *Reichsmarschall* raises his glass to Laval, Petain and Darlan, members of the Vichy government, as a downbeat Mussolini plays the part of waiter, 1943. Artist Artur Szyk shows Goering feasting on US relief rations while blood drips from a list of the names of hostages shot in France

WAR IS COMING

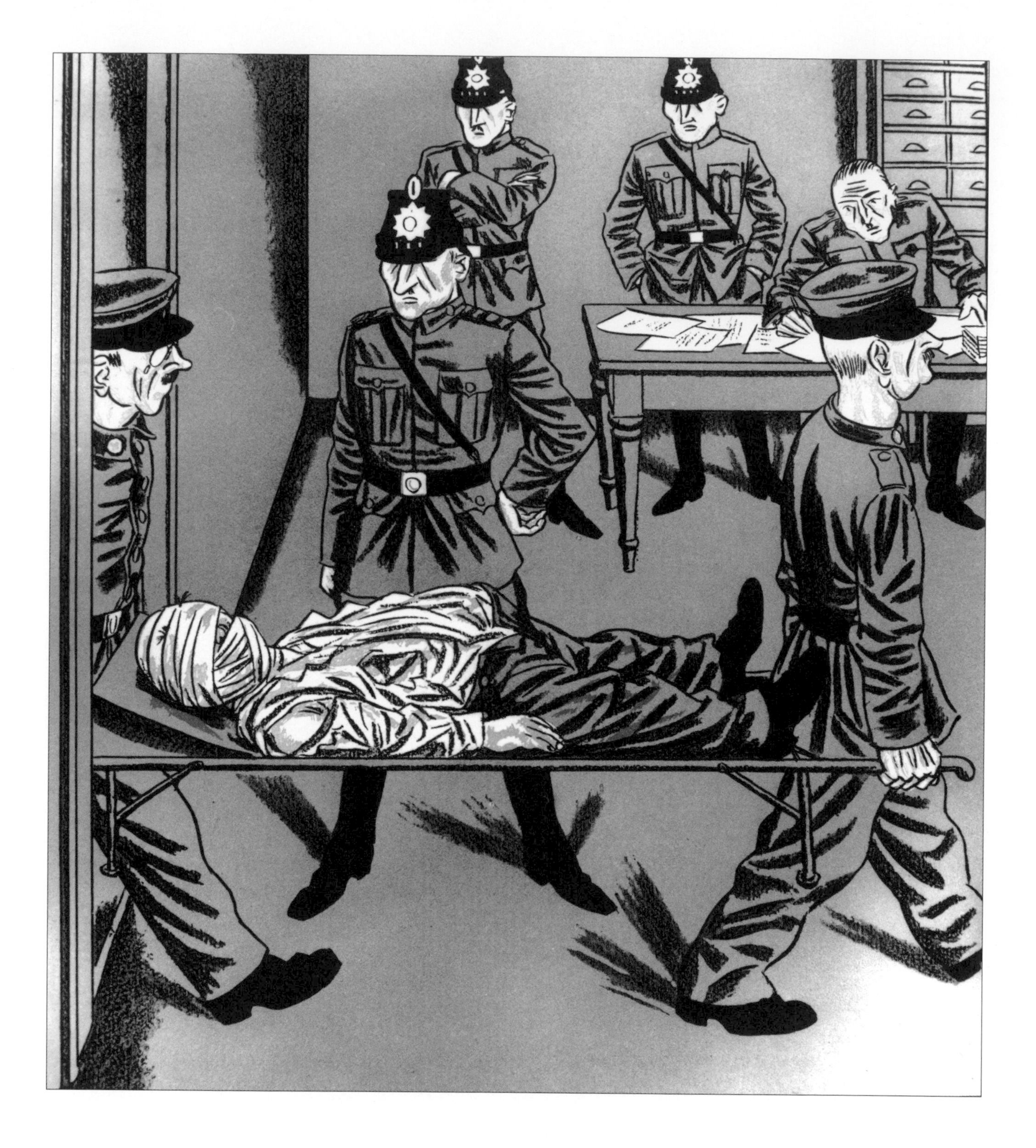

A cartoon, probably by Thomas Theodor Heine, from Munich satirical magazine *Simplicissimus* (1927) which shows a wounded man being carried into a police station: 'Berlin on Sunday. Was he run over by a car?' 'No, he ran into the National-Socialists.'

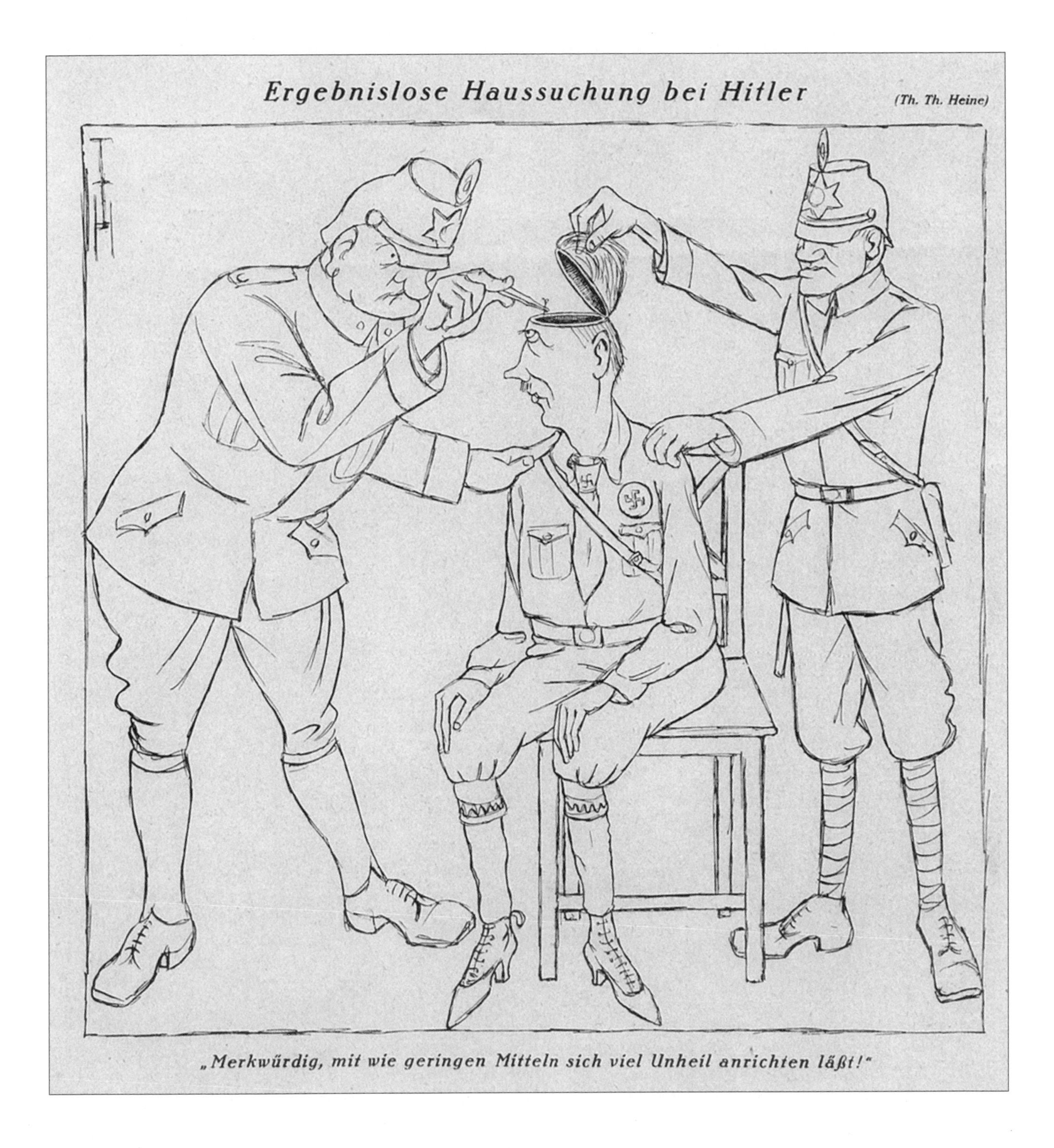

'Inconclusive Search at Hitler's Place – remarkable how much disaster has grown from so tiny a seed' – by Th. Th. Heine, as he signed himself, 1930. The artist fled Germany for Prague in 1933

Colonel Blimp, drawn by David Low for London's *Evening Standard* newspaper, was a stereotypical British figure of the 1930s, lampooned for his dim, jingoistic views. In 1943, Churchill tried to stop the making of a film about Blimp by Powell and Pressburger because the script had made the main German character too sympathetic

‘How Mr Hitler says “legal”’(1932): in 1930 Hitler promised the National Court in Leipzig that the Nazis would keep within the law. When he became Chancellor, he systematically subverted Germany’s legal system, so he could do as he liked

'Hitler – Our Last Hope' by Mjölnir (Hans Schweitzer), 1932. With 6 million unemployed and weaknesses in the constitution that crippled the government, Hitler was happy to present himself as Germany's saviour for the upcoming elections

'Marxism is the guardian angel of capitalism. Vote Nazi', 1932: a typically anti-semitic Nazi poster shows an effete Marxist-Social Democrat angel hand in hand with a Jewish businessman in a world where swastikas have replaced the stars

A prescient image by Georges that appeared in *The Nation*, New York on 5 April 1933, suggesting the reality that lay behind Hitler's mask

'Changing Directions', 1933, by H. Wolfe, shows Germany being sidetracked from peace by the Nazis and embarking on a route that leads to war, murder, tears, suffering and destruction

'The Partitioning of the World' by Russian artist Boris Yefimov – Germany gets Europe and Japan takes Asia, 1934

'The Rise of Hitler' by French artist Ralph Soupault from the publication *Charivari*, 1933

'Not the Most Comfortable Seat' from the *Chicago Daily News*, March 1933. Hitler had been elected Chancellor of Germany on 6 March, and many outside observers believed he would not be up to the job of dealing with German economic woes and the forces of militarism

Der Stürmer

Deutsches Wochenblatt zum Kampfe um die Wahrheit

HERAUSGEBER : JULIUS STREICHER

Nummer 9 | Nürnberg im März 1934 | 12. Jahr 1934

Mörder Alljuda

Der geheimnisvolle Tod des Richters Prince

Der Staviskyskandal

Vor einigen Wochen wurde in Frankreich ein un- eheurer Bestechungsskandal aufgedeckt. In seinem Mit- elpunkt stand der Jude **Stavisky**. Parlamentarier, Se- atoren, Bürgermeister, höchste Beamte und Minister varen seine Komplizen. Der **Stavisky**-Skandal zog ge- valtige Folgen nach sich. In allen Städten Frankreichs anden riesige Demonstrationen statt. Zwei Kabinette rachten zusammen. In der Kammer verprügelten sich die Abgeordneten. Auf den Straßen und Plätzen ballte ich die in namenlose Wut geratene Bevölkerung zu- ammen. Tote und Schwerverwundete deckten das Pfla- ter. Das Volk stand auf gegen die Regierung und gegen einen bis in die Knochen verlumpten Parlamen- arismus.

Inzwischen ist man daran die Barrikaden aufzuräu- nen, verbrannte Autos abzuschleppen und die Aufruhr- chäden auszubessern. Eine verdächtige Stille liegt über Paris. Die Stille vor dem Sturm. Die schuldbeladenen Parteiführer schlottern immer noch vor Angst. Höchste Ministerialbeamte sehen sorgenvoll in die Zukunft. Dicke Parlamentarier, Bank- und Börsenjuden ducken sich ängst- ich. Allen ist eine Frage ins Gesicht geschrieben: Wann kommt der zweite Schlag? Alle drückt das Gauner- gewissen. Alle haben sie Dreck am Stecken und bangen vor der Stunde, die alle Schuldigen im **Stavisky**-Skandal entlarven wird. Sie sehen sich schon aus ihren Woh- nungen geholt, durch die Straßen geschleift, irgendwo winkt ein Galgen. Furchtbare Gesichter quälen die Schma- rotzer der französischen Republik.

Die Furcht vor Prince

Alle hassen sie einen Mann. Der kennt ihre Schand- taten. Er hat sie in seiner Hand. Wenn er den Mund öffnet, reißt sie der Strudel mit. Der Strudel, der Namen und Reichtum verschlingt. Der ins Zuchthaus führt. Der Mann heißt **Prince**. Er ist Ratsmitglied des Pariser Appellationsgerichtshofes. Er ist Richter an jenem Gericht, in dem das Material des **Stavisky**- Skandales zu Bergen anwächst. So weit man ihn kennt, wird dieser gerade, pflichtbewußte **Prince** den Mund auf- tun. Und ohne Ansehen der Person die Schuldigen zur Rechenschaft ziehen. „Besticht ihn!" raten die einen. Ihn wird Geld nie zum Schweigen bringen können. Einer sagt es plötzlich, was alle denken: **Prince muß stumm gemacht werden für immer. Er muß sterben!**

Freimaurer

Die halbe Welt im Irrenwahn, ist Judas Zielen untertan
vor Mord wird nicht zurückgeschreckt, was is schon, wenn ä Goi verreckt

Aus dem Inhalt

- Nationalsozialismus in Polen
- Die Tochter des Lokomotivführers
- Jud Neuhöfer unschädlich gemacht
- Kußtänze mit Juden im Spessart
- Brief aus der Schweiz

Die Juden sind unser Unglück!

The front page of Nazi rag *Der Stürmer*, from March 1934, with a cartoon by regular cartoonist Fips (Philipp Rupprecht), complete with one of his trademark anti-semitic, anti-freemasonic cartoons – two scapegoats for the price of one!

'The German people know: the greater the need, the stronger the Führer will be': this morale-boosting image by Arthur Johnson was produced after the Night of the Long Knives, when having suppressed his enemies, Hitler had arrested over 800 of his Nazi critics, about 90 of whom were killed

British Foreign Secretary Anthony Eden stands bemused at the main players in the Spanish Civil War and how they might be lining up for conflicts to come, *Punch* 1936

This German propaganda cartoon mocks Churchill for believing he could rely on women to protect him from the Germans (date unknown)

'Hitler with Halo': this was a cover drawn by Sennep (Jean Pennes) for French satirical magazine *Le Rire*, 1934. Sennep fought for the French Cavalry in World War I and later worked for *Le Figaro* where he became one of the greatest anti-Hitler cartoonists

'The Accused' by ultra-nationalist French artist Paul Iribe, 1934: Marianne, symbol of France, is being judged by the great powers, represented by Ramsay MacDonald, Hitler, Mussolini and Roosevelt. Iribe blamed sneering and bullying foreigners for the political turmoil in France, along with homegrown politicians of course. Iribe was the lover of Coco Chanel, here the model for Marianne

ADOLF IN THE LOOKING-GLASS.

HERR HITLER. "HOW FRIGHTFUL I LOOK TO-DAY!"

This image was produced in 1934 by Bernard Partridge and is evidence of how anxious the British were becoming at the turn of events in Germany

1935 and the shadow of Germany's past and present looms large over delegates at the League of Nations – Hitler withdrew Germany from that organization in 1933. This image by Paul Iribe appeared in the polemical journal *Le Témoin* (The Witness), which he founded with the financial backing of Coco Chanel

THE GOOSE-STEP

"GOOSEY GOOSEY GANDER,
WHITHER DOST THOU WANDER?"
"ONLY THROUGH THE RHINELAND—
PRAY EXCUSE MY BLUNDER!"

This drawing, by E.H. Shepard, is a comment on the remilitarization of the Rhineland amid German demands for further expansion. The goose is stepping all over a torn Treaty of Locarno. This document was drawn up to preserve national borders

DELAYED ACTION.

"I WONDER HOW MUCH LONGER I CAN KEEP THIS ATTITUDE UP WITHOUT LETTING THE THING GO?"

Bernard Partridge used the 1936 Berlin Olympics to highlight Hitler's refusal to reveal exactly what he had in mind for Europe

Japanese forces attacked China as a new power arose in the East – by Bernard Partridge, 1937. The rising sun with radiating rays was the main image on the official war flag of the Japanese army at this time

LITTLE CZECH-RIDING-HOOD

"What sharp teeth you have, Grandmamma!"
"All the better for peacefully revising treaties, my dear."

As the Sudeten Crisis of 1938 unfolded, cartoonist Bernard Partridge mocked Hitler's claim to want to redraw Germany's border with Czechoslovakia by peaceful means and highlighted the futility of the Czech offer of concessions

In 1938, Stalin was still seen as the arch-enemy by Nazi artist Erich Schilling in *Simplicissimus* – here, the Russian dictator is complaining about grave-diggers joining the general strike in Paris. He wouldn't ever allow such a thing himself: grave-digging was far too important for the future of Bolshevism

'Take Me to Czechoslovakia, Driver': Hermann Goering called this cartoon by Vaughn Shoemaker 'a horrible example of anti-Nazi propaganda' – from the *Chicago Times*, 1938

Pont (Graham Laidler) captured the mood of the time as the British found it increasingly hard to ignore what was happening in Europe; opposite page: he also imagined what might be going on in the minds of the Germans

THE BRITISH CHARACTER

Tendency to keep out of foreign politics

". . . I am beginning to think I have been letting things worry me too much lately, because . . ."

(In Germany) The English

(In Germany) The Germans

1939

THE GATHERING OF THE VULTURES

["The whole great Central European area, of which the Bohemian valley and lands are only a segment, will be renovated through the political will of the Fuehrer."—*German Paper*.]

Bernard Partridge re-imagined the topographical map of Central Europe

THE CRYSTAL-GAZER

Watched by the shade of Germany's past, Hitler peers into his crystal ball and does not flinch at what he sees – by Bernard Partridge

'Appeasement': a tightrope-walking Neville Chamberlain, then Prime Minister, complete with trademark umbrella, is about to come a cropper as British prestige begins to unravel – by New Zealand artist Don Angus

Pen and ink representation of the Nazis' invasion of Poland by Jerzy Faczynski, who escaped to England in 1939 to fight for the Polish free forces. In the Bible, the Fourth Horseman of the Apocalypse was Death riding on a pale horse

THE TWO CONSTRICTORS

"I don't know about helping you, Adolf, but I *do* understand your point of view!"

Who's the bigger snake? Bernard Partridge sees through the marriage of convenience between the Nazis and the Soviet Union

David Low also decides there isn't much to choose between Stalin and Hitler. As early as 1936, British diplomats began to receive complaints from Germany about New Zealand-born cartoonist Low's drawings of Hitler. They were really getting under the Führer's skin. During review sessions of the foreign press, Hitler would explode with rage when he saw the artist's latest work. Low was said to be high on the Nazi death list to be implemented once Britain was conquered

Legendary US cartoonist Clifford Berryman added his voice to the widespread mockery of the Russo-German non-aggression pact

Hitler and Mussolini are sowing the fields of Europe with guns and tanks, but 'what will their harvest be?' – by Paul Ordner in French satirical weekly *Le Rire*

München, 17. September 1939
44. Jahrgang / Nummer 37
30 Pfennig

SIMPLICISSIMUS

VERLAG KNORR & HIRTH KOMMANDITGESELLSCHAFT, MÜNCHEN

Die alte englische Methode

(E. Thöny)

„Das hat Old Churchill wieder mal gut gemacht: kaum ist der Krieg ausgebrochen, läßt er die Athenia sinken und schon sind die Deutschen daran schuld. Gelernt ist eben gelernt."

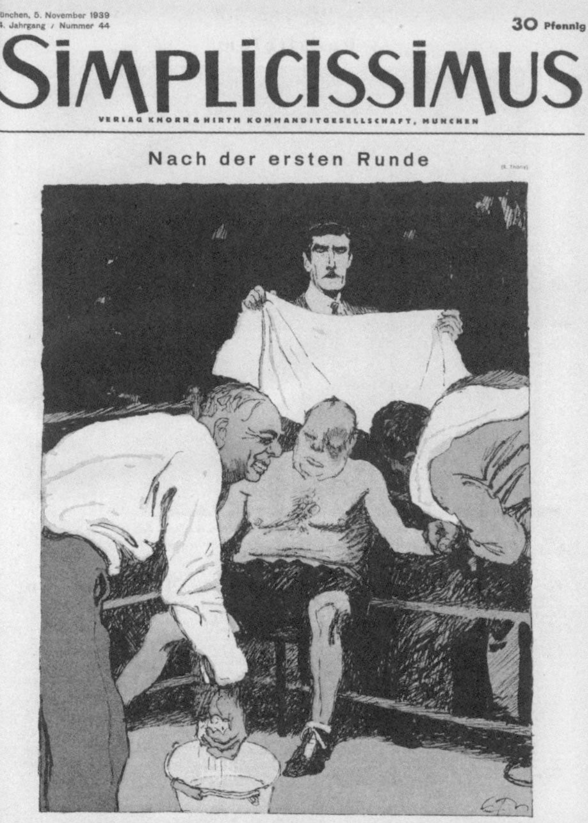

München, 5. November 1939
44. Jahrgang / Nummer 44
30 Pfennig

SIMPLICISSIMUS

VERLAG KNORR & HIRTH KOMMANDITGESELLSCHAFT, MÜNCHEN

Nach der ersten Runde

Churchill mußte mehrere schwere Treffer einstecken. Erste Runde einwandfrei für uns!

München, 26. November 1939
44. Jahrgang / Nummer 47
30 Pfennig

SIMPLICISSIMUS

VERLAG KNORR & HIRTH KOMMANDITGESELLSCHAFT, MÜNCHEN

Churchill — Fallstaff

(Karl Arnold)

„Kriegsgründe sind für mich so wohlfeil wie Brombeeren!"

Simplicissimus was Germany's top satirical magazine, which turned right-wing under the Nazis. Here are three covers from 1939 with (from the top) the view from the old fellows on a park bench, pointing out 'England's traditional habit of blaming the Germans for everything'; Churchill, then First Lord of the Admiralty, taking a pummelling in the first round of the naval war; a drunken Churchill as Falstaff

'The Enemy is on the Prowl for Your Secrets': Paul Colin was one of France's greatest poster artists. He helped launch the career of his lover Josephine Baker with his poster for *Revue Nègre* in 1925 and produced just shy of 2,000 posters during his lifetime

Above: 'The Stoker' – Hitler shovels more corpses into the furnace as the Germans burn their way across Europe – by Philip Zec in Britain's *Daily Mirror*; left: Marshall Petain brings Marianne of France to Vichy for a health cure, courtesy of *Der Stürmer*; opposite: 'The Campaign of Lies – the Democracies have called on their most loyal troops to encircle Germany.' Ducks are a German metaphor for lies, a *Zeitungsente* being a false story in a newspaper, and here they are seen emerging from Jewish lips. Vile anti-semitism was the default setting in Nazi newspapers and magazines

Der Lügenfeldzug
(Erich Schilling)
Die Demokratien haben ihre treuesten Truppen restlos mobilisiert, um Deutschland einzukreisen!

THE CALL TO TRAINING

A cheerful *Punch* cartoon in which a queue of John Bulls and Britannias is transformed into a column of patriotic volunteers for the auxiliary services – by Leslie Illingworth

WINGS FROM THE WEST

Although the USA did not officially join the war until Pearl Harbor in 1941, it provided aid and military assistance as soon as the arms embargo had been lifted – by E.H. Shepard

Life in the B.E.F.

"Gosh! Aren't you sick and tired of all these silly jokes about the black-out?"

Pont always sought to downplay the gravity of any situation, gently sending up the character of the British at the same time. The cartoon (above) is a reference to a popular song of 1939, 'We're Going to Hang Out the Washing on the Siegfried Line', written by Captain James Kennedy, then serving in the British Expeditionary Force in the sector opposite the German defensive works known as the Siegfried Line

"I remind you of who*?" I said. And then I knocked the blighter down."*

"Must you say 'Well, we're still here' every morning?"

THE WOODEN DOVE

"It came to me in a nightmare, Hermann—my secret weapon against the Allies for next year's campaign."

Hitler explains his brilliant new plan to Hermann Goering. This drawing by Bernard Partridge appeared in *Punch*

THE HAND OF PROVIDENCE

"If that doesn't make him more popular, his next escape must be narrower still."

This cartoon by E.H. Shepard commemorates Johann Georg Elser's attempt to assassinate Adolf Hitler in a Munich beer cellar – Hitler left 13 minutes before the bomb went off. Elser was also planning to kill Hitler's jealous comrades Goering and Goebbels

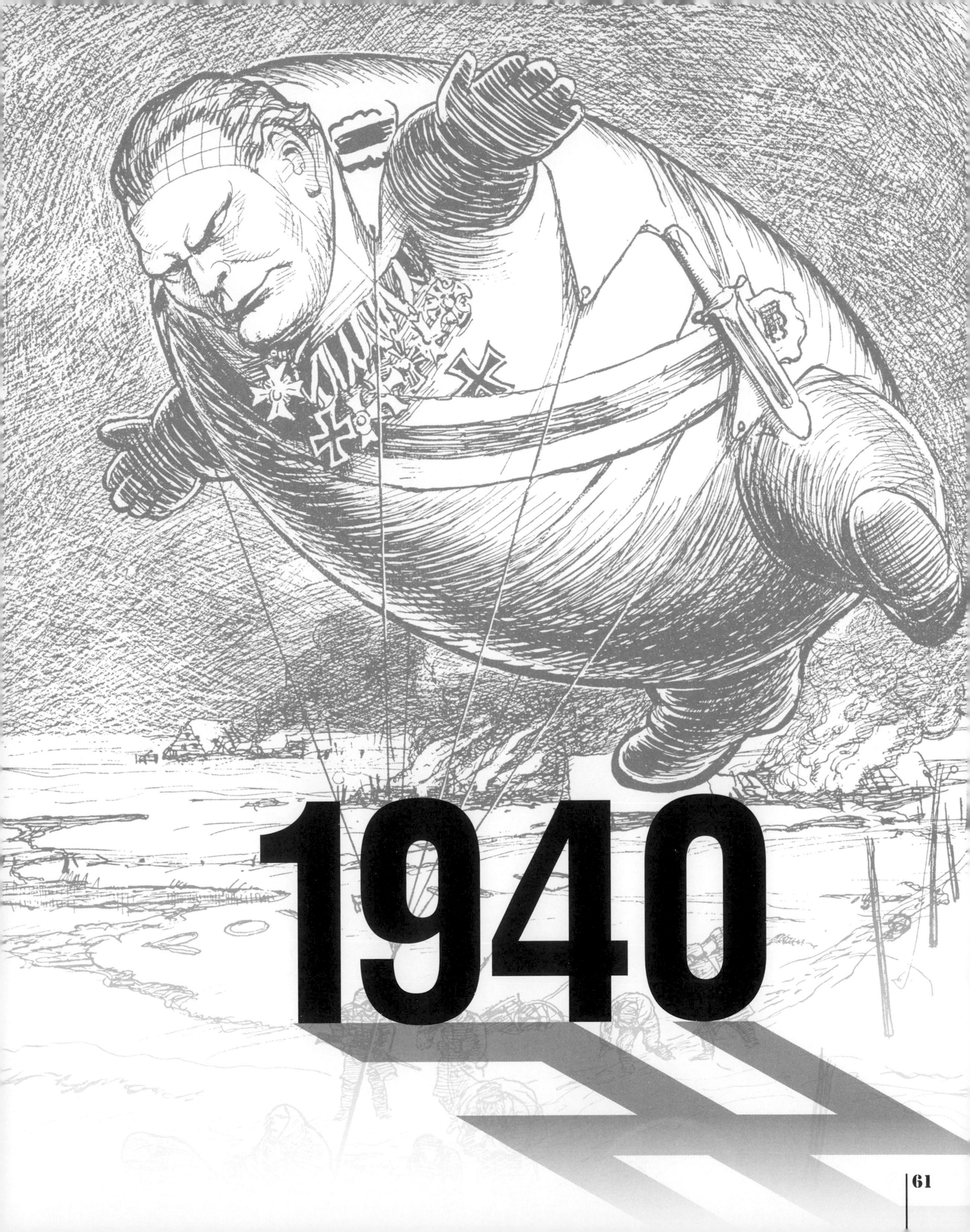

1940

Above: 'The Floor gets hot: the dance on the volcanoes begins!': anti-British cartoon by Bogner in *Das Schwarze Korps*, the magazine of the SS; left: 'The Cry for help to Freemasonry': John Bull: 'Help. Help.' Freemason: 'Man, the water is right up to my… trowel', also by Bogner in *Das Schwarze Korps*; right: 'peacemaker' Neville Chamberlain and 'warmonger' Churchill lament the disaster at Dunkirk in this piece of German propaganda. Across the water, British propagandists put their minds to the task of turning defeat at Dunkirk into victory of a kind for domestic consumption

W.C

'Peaceful Penetration': a warning to US isolationists that the Nazis were capable of threatening interests in America's backyard – by Pulitzer Prize winner J.N. ('Ding') Darling

Hitler and Stalin wash their dirty linen in public but, try as they might, they can't remove the bloodstains from Austria, Czechoslovakia, Poland and Finland. Drawing by Paul Ordner first published in *Marianne* magazine

FREEDOM

A single Spitfire stands between the British and disaster as it takes on the German juggernaut in this memorable drawing by Leslie Illingworth for *Punch*

Above: 'The Terrible problems of the Upper Classes Somewhere in England – Your Majesty, there is no other choice, you just have to swallow it [socialism]' from *Das Reich*. Josef Goebbels wrote the editorials for this 'upmarket' weekly; left: French artist Sennep has Mussolini attempting to sell his mother's sexual favours to Hitler

MAN AGAINST THE MACHINE.

'Man Against the Machine' by Pulitzer Prize winner
Daniel Fitzpatrick in the *St. Louis Post-Dispatch*

'The Fifth Horseman of the Apocalypse' by Daniel Fitzpatrick, whose powerful body of work played an important part in making the US rethink its isolationist stance towards Europe; right: in *De Robot* by L.J. Jordaan, the German automaton marches unstoppably across Holland. This was first published in an underground newspaper called *De Groene Amsterdammer*

JORDAAN

'The Bloodbath' shows the British betraying their French allies as a typical Tommy takes his French counterpart to the brink, then laughingly takes a step backwards as monsieur dives into the bloodbath alone. This is a German propaganda strip by Oskar Garvens, who produced a very similar work about the Russian betrayal of the Germans, also called 'The Bloodbath'

MILITARY OBJECTIVES

"Once again these inhuman British our helpless munition factories have bombed, instead of concentrating on women and children, as is the way of the glorious Reich!"

E.H. Shepard's drawing of a cowardly Goebbels and Goering serves two purposes, reminding us of the cruelty and viciousness of the Nazis as well as portraying British bombing as being increasingly effective

Seeing spies

Pont (Graham Laidler)

One of the great chroniclers of the British way of life, Graham Laidler was born in 1908 in Jesmond, Newcastle upon Tyne. His family moved to the south of England after the premature death of his father and Laidler began training at the London School of Architecture, but was never able to take up this profession after he was diagnosed with tuberculosis in 1932. He was, however, able to put his draughtsmanship to good use.

Under the pseudonym of Pont (short for *Pontifex Maximus*, the high priest in Ancient Rome), he became a cartoonist for *Punch* magazine where his keen eye was put to use in observing the foibles of his fellow countrymen. His best work was as gentle as it was subtle.

Pont was a master of understatement. In 'Seeing spies', above, he seems to suggest that, when you come to think about it, anyone could be a spy. Or, opposite above, he shows a family gathering on top of their Anderson shelter in order to get a better view of a bombing raid. Perhaps the most famous Pont drawing is the pub, opposite below, where life carries on regardless, despite the imminent possibility of invasion by the Nazis.

Pont died of poliomyelitis at the age of 32 in 1940 when Britain was undergoing nightly bombardment at the hands of the Luftwaffe and the Nazi High Command were training their sights across the Channel. Pont is commemorated by the Pont Award for cartoonists who reflect 'the British Character'.

". . . Meanwhile, in Britain, the entire population faced by the threat of invasion, has been flung into a state of complete panic . . . etc., etc., etc."

Uncle Frederic at 8.32 p.m. last Tuesday—if his description is strictly in accordance with the facts.

"My dear fellow, we had a land mine slap through the roof."

"It's remarkably quiet—I wonder if anything's wrong."

". . . and not only decorative, they're loaded."

'Teutonic Warrior Knight' perfectly captures the genius of Josef Goebbels in the dark arts of propaganda – as well as similar attributes in artist David Low

‘Dinner for Two’: Mussolini begs for scraps at Hitler’s table and is given the wishbone as consolation – by Ferman Martin of the *Houston Chronicle*. When France surrendered to Germany and Italy in June 1940, Hitler took two entire provinces from France for Germany, but gave Italy only a few pockets of land in the Alps

THE GREAT PROTECTOR

[Field-Marshal Goering has confiscated all property in Poland "in order to safeguard it."]

E.H. Shepard pictured Goering as a barrage balloon, bloated with what he had consumed, hovering menacingly above the war-torn landscape of Poland

WHO AIDS?

Little Finland prepares to protect itself as the spectre of the Soviet Union, armed with hammer and sickle, looms over its border

'Old Bill and Co': at the height of a German air-raid, the British ARP warden is shouting down the chimney, 'I said, I reckon it's time you went to the shelter.' British artist Bruce Bairnsfather was hospitalized with shell shock after the Battle of Ypres in World War I and served as official cartoonist to the US Army in Europe during World War II

" Don't stand there knocking, Roberts, GO STRAIGHT IN."

In 1940, Britain was taking
a battering from the Luftwaffe;
this cartoon by Hewitt shows
a forgetful British fire warden
observing the usual proprieties in a
situation where they are no longer
remotely useful

READING THE SKIES.

"I have conquered all Gaul. How long will it take to conquer all Britain?"
"Wait a moment, Leader, while I look at the omens of the air."

E.H. Shepard cast Hitler as a Roman emperor to Goebbels' fawning seer as the Battle of Britain raged overhead, complete with a schoolboy joke in bad Latin

DELAYED ACTION

"It's from Benito. He wants to know whether you've polished off those contemptible British—because if so he's ready to defy the full strength of Greece."

Divide and rule: Bernard Partridge sought to tickle up discord within the ranks of the Axis powers by pointing out the feeble contribution of the Italian armed forces

Hitler was supposed to have worked as a house painter in Munich and this idea provided inspiration for a number of wartime cartoonists, including Neil Lonsdale in the *New Zealand Observer*

I first heard old Mrs. Todd at the post office telling somebody—

then Mr. Brewis told me himself;

Miss Greer came out with the same story—

and I thought little Miss Hopstead was going to take a fit when she told me.

Doctor Gregory had a completely different version of the same thing—

and as for Admiral Stoker . . .

Col. Chargem and his friend could talk of nothing else—

Young Whatshisname was full of it—

so were the people in the bank.

The Vicar was booming about it all over the place—

and Mrs. Trent had, as usual, got the whole thing mixed up.

Vera Prestwood said her father had gone to bed immediately when he heard it—

But old Clogwheels said he had expected worse.

Frank ran right across the road to tell me—

and even the people at the Wilsons' wanted to know what I thought.

But I am not going to tell YOU *what it was, because I never repeat rumours.*

The Saturday morning rumour.

Rumours spread like wildfire during wartime. Pont liked the idea of showing how a rumour spread, but preferred to tease the reader as to what that rumour might have been

A German vampire feasts on the blood of the Dutch in this stunning image by Leendert Jurriaan Jordaan

British poster warning people to watch what they said 'on the blower' as the telephone was then known

WITH THE GREATEST OF EASE?

'With the Greatest of Ease?' by Vaughn Shoemaker in the *Chicago Daily News* – taking the words from a popular song of the time, Shoemaker noted Hitler's unhindered progress through northern Europe, implying that the Balkans were next and that the world had better do something about it

1941

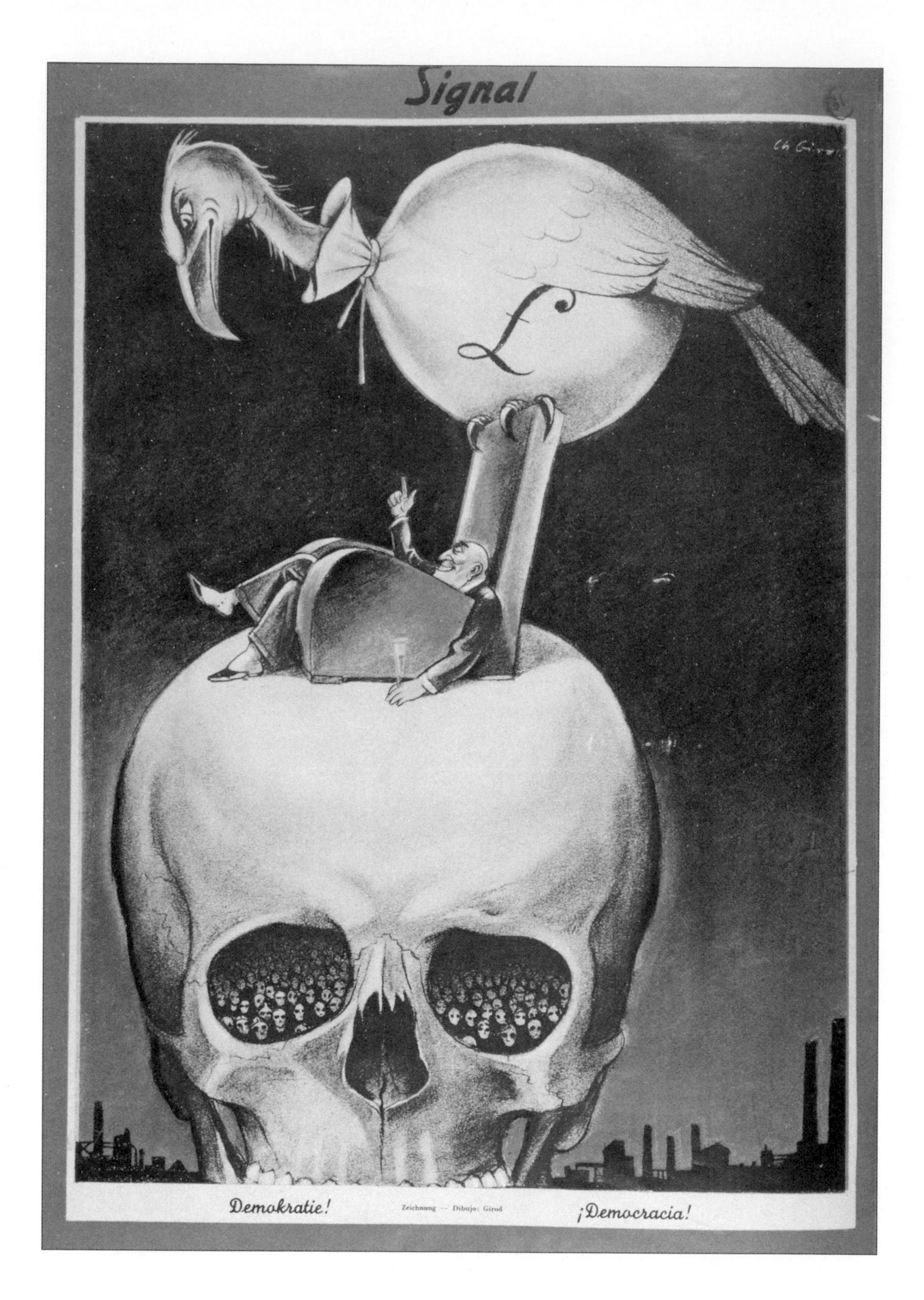

Signal was a glossy propaganda magazine produced by the Wehrmacht for distribution throughout occupied Europe. At its height, the circulation was a heady 2.5 million in around 30 languages. This image is entitled 'Democracy!'

‘Instead of Soprano’: Josef Goebbels was rumoured to have had an affair with soprano Elisabeth Schwarzkopf and there’s no doubt he was intent on turning culture into a propaganda tool of the Nazi state. None of this escaped the vigilance of the Kukryniksy group of cartoonists in Russia

Down Lover's Lane. *Hitler wooed Stalin . . . but with large forces stationed right on Russia's doorstep* **(June 17, 1941)**

On 22 June 1941, under the codename 'Operation Barbarossa', Germany invaded Russia – Hitler had always regarded the pact between Germany and Russia as short term and just about everyone could see the break-up coming from a mile off, including Philip Zec in the *Daily Mirror*

'Hitler's Barbershop': the Führer only cuts hair one way – by legendary US cartoonist Clifford Berryman

'Let's Destroy the Enemy Mercilessly!': Kukryniksy liked to go straight for the jugular in the 74 posters they produced for Moscow's TASS studio during the 'Great Patriotic War'. This was perhaps one of their more restrained efforts

‘The Face of Hitlerism’ by Viktor Deni. Deni worked for *Pravda*, the Communist Party daily, but returned to making posters during World War II, a task he had previously performed during the Bolshevik revolution

Though racially prejudiced—I would like to know how you crossed the Red Sea?

A subtle effort from Czechoslovak cartoonist Stephen (Stephen Roth) as Britain faced invasion, part of a book called *Jesters in Earnest* published in wartime Britain with a preface by David Low. This is a dig at Hitler's inability to cross the English Channel to invade Britain

German soldiers! Enjoy your leave and return to the front in good health and high spirits.
(Goebbels).

This was Stephen's take on the realities facing Germany despite the encouraging words to the troops from Josef Goebbels. The image contains some rewarding details

'Struwwelhitler': the front cover of a book written in parody of *Struwwelpeter*, a collection of cautionary stories for children compiled with a cruel Germanic edge. Here, the inside pages featured Mussolini, Goebbels and other favourites

Kladderdatsch was a satirical magazine founded in 1848. When it was taken over by industrialist Hugo Stinnes in 1923 it shifted increasingly to the right. This cover by Arthur Johnson shows Churchill licking Roosevelt's boots just after the USA had entered the war – the artist's father was American but he was brought up in Germany by his mother

This was a leaflet dropped by Japanese pilots over Pearl Harbor. Crudely phrased, it was reproduced on duplicating machines using rough foolscap. The Japanese lettering says, 'Listen to the voice of doom. Open your eyes, blind fools'

Poster inviting 'talented young men' to join the Chinese air force – part of a propaganda campaign by the occupying Japanese

'Adolf the Wolf': Dr Seuss (Theodor Seuss Geisel) was a prolific political cartoonist during World War II; he was highly critical of American isolationism

'Pepper Soup': Hitler finds his alphabet soup, with the names of Nazi sympathizers spelt out in it, has been spoiled after the speech of Florida senator Pepper in support of joining the Allied cause – by Lynn Brudon

Kukryniksy

Kukryniksy was the name adopted by three Russian caricaturists, Mikhail Kuprilianov, Porfirii Krylov and Nokolai Sokolov, who met at the newly established VKHUTEMAS art school, Moscow, in the 1920s. Inspired by the atmosphere of revolutionary fervour, they adopted their collective name in 1924 and ditched the parochialism that had previously characterized their work. There was a job to be done for the USSR.

Kukryniksy learned how to apply their keen sense of the grotesque to political subjects and they became rising stars of Soviet publications such as *Krokodil* and *Pravda*. Maxim Gorky stepped forward to encourage them and their acidic portraits of Hitler, Mussolini, Franco and other fascists became increasingly merciless…

During World War II, they produced over 70 posters for the TASS studio in Moscow and, after the war, they were sent to document the Nuremberg trials by *Pravda*. Kukryniksy produced vital propaganda used to spur on the Soviet war effort and won the Stalin Prize five times, along with the Lenin Prize (1965) and the State Prize of the USSR (1975).

Above: 'Cannibal Vegetarian': another vicious skit on Hitler, contrasting his treatment of animals and human beings; opposite: the image top left is by Boris Yefimov, the others are all by Kukryniksy

IMPROVING THE RACE
Selected breed of delegates for Nazi Congress
Cartoon by Yefimov, 1941

FIB-DETECTORS
German Command's Report of Military Operations
Cartoon by Kukryniksy, 1941

ARABIAN TALES
Cartoon by Kukryniksy, 1941

THE NAZI KENNEL
Cartoon by Kukryniksy, 1941

"Therefore, he resolved to venture and hold his ground."

Leslie Illingworth quoted John Bunyan's *The Pilgrim's Progress* and neatly captured the mood in Britain, where resolve was practically all that was available to vanquish a monstrous foe

The work of artist Rowland Emett proved that, even in the direst circumstances, the British still had time for gentle gags, as a circus elephant gets mixed up with a convoy of tanks in the English countryside

"Actually this is now very much as Wren INTENDED *us to see St. Paul's."*

This cartoon by W.A. Sillince in *Punch* captured the spirit of the Blitz: forget the damage caused by German bombing, St Paul's now symbolized that the British would survive whatever was thrown at them

THE COMMON TASK

Also in *Punch*, Leslie Illingworth pictured an older man quietly but determinedly digging for victory as British warships steam past

CANADA
1942

'New Order': the Nazis wished to impose a 'new order' on Europe and this cartoon by Boris Yefimov highlights the trail of death in countries that had been incorporated into the Third Reich: Denmark, Norway, France, Italy, Czechoslovakia, Greece, Yugoslavia, Romania and Poland

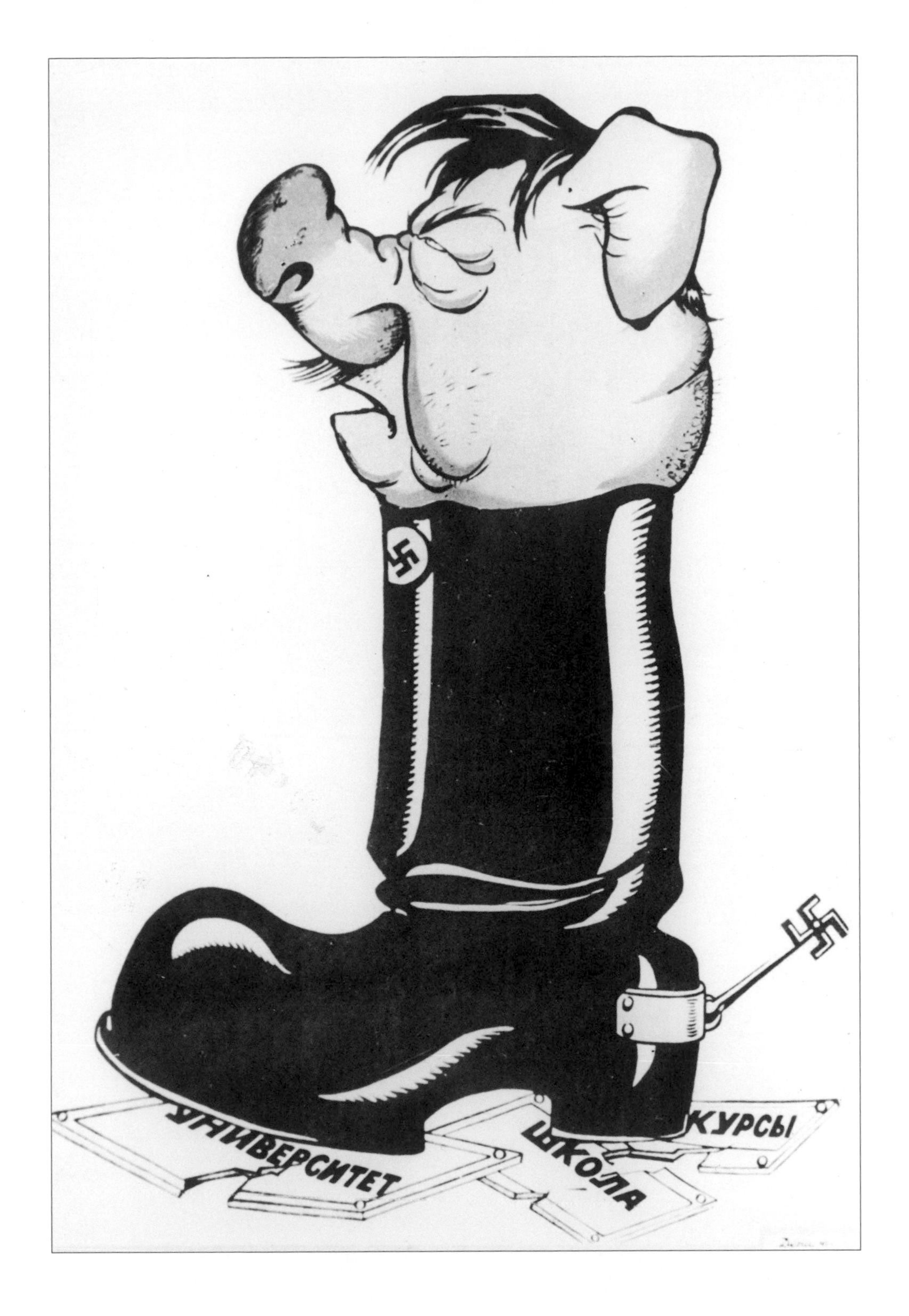

Russian poster specialist Viktor Deni derided Hitler as an ignorant pig stuffed into a jackboot: 'University, School, Courses… What use has a pig for culture and science? Its horizon is extremely narrow. *Mein Kampf* is its highest achievement…'

"By the way, I managed to get some corned beef for dinner."

Above: Mervyn Wilson's comment on wartime shortages from *Punch*; opposite above, 'Flagday for the Eastern Front' by Stephen, a satirical view of how the war was going on the home front in Germany; below: 'We're fighting for culture, Jimmy', a racist Nazi leaflet mocking black US troops. (The response – 'But what is culture?' – is missing on this version of the cartoon, as is the title, 'Liberators')

Flagday for the Eastern Front.

„Wir kämpfen für das Kultur, Jimmy."

Churchills Morgengymnastik

(Erich Schilling)

„Wer hätte gedacht, daß ich einmal diese tiefen Rumpfbeugen machen müßte, um meine Figur zu behalten!“

Ginnastica mattutina di Churchill: "Chi mai avrebbe pensato che io un giorno, per mantenere la mia figura, avrei dovuto fare queste profonde flessioni di torso!,,

Ihnen, entsetzliche Angst. Ich habe seither keine Nacht mehr geschlafen. Ich stellte mir Sie vor als einen Mann mit ungeheuren Fäusten und wildem Blick. Ach, Gott sei Dank ... Gott sei Dank! ... Verzeihen Sie, ich kann Ihnen nichts anbieten. Vielleicht eine von den Zigarren meines Mannes. Ich erinnere mich, daß er eine gute Sorte rauchte ..."

Sie trippelte eilig zu der Kommode und brachte ein vergilbtes Kistchen, in dem einige halb entblätterte Henry Clay mit rot und goldenen Ringen lagen. Nachdem Herr Wranitzky sich, wie es in der Gesellschaft des ancien regime gebräuchlich gewesen war, entsprechend gesträubt hatte, nahm er die Zigarre und erhob sich. Denn der Hund wurde schon ungeduldig. Es wurde taktvoll vermieden, die Hundefrage nochmals zu berühren. Er verließ das Haus. Der Hund tänzelte freudig bellend vor ihm her. Herr Wranitzky begrub das Kriegsbeil und begann eine Wohnung in pinscherfreier Gegend zu suchen. Manchmal, wenn er sich seines Feldzuges gegen die Gesandtin erinnerte, dachte er, daß mancher Streit im kleinen wie im großen vermieden werden könnte, wenn jeder sich bemühen würde, den Feind kennenzulernen und seine Not zu verstehn.

326

'Churchill's Morning Exercises – Who'd have thought that I'd have to keep bending over like this to keep my figure!' – drawn by Erich Schilling for *Simplicissimus*

München, 30. Dezember 1942
47. Jahrgang / Nummer 53

30 Pfennig

SIMPLICISSIMUS

VERLAG KNORR & HIRTH KOMMANDITGESELLSCHAFT, MÜNCHEN

Churchill am Neujahrsmorgen

(Erich Schilling)

„Bist du noch der Britenlöwe, oder schon der große amerikanische Kater?"

'Churchill on New Year's Day – Are you the British lion… or the big American tom-cat?' (*Kater* also means a hangover in German.) Schilling loved his New Year's messages to Churchill, but by winning the war Churchill had the last word. The artist killed himself in 1945

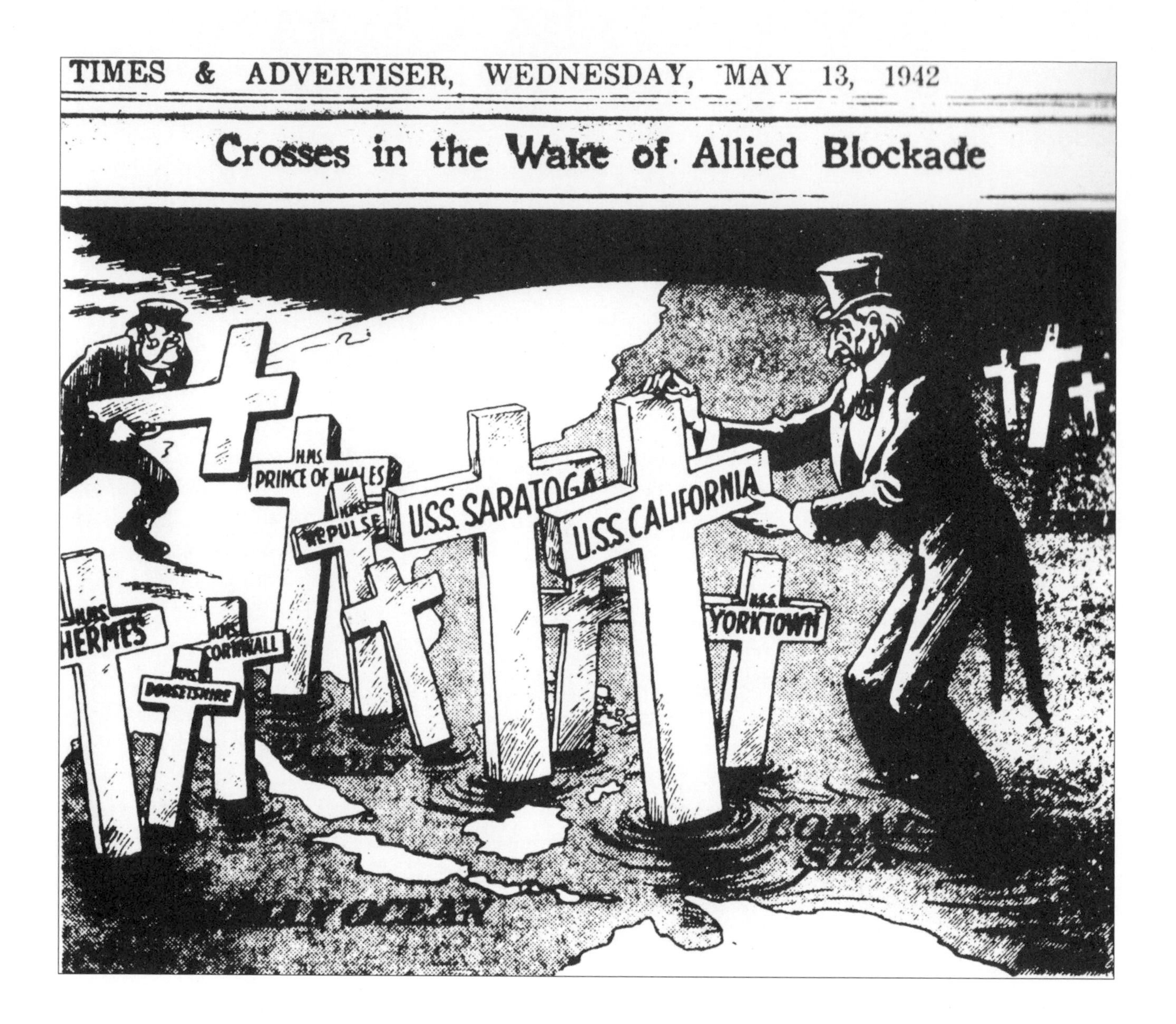

Propaganda image from the Japanese English-language newspaper *Japan Times & Advertiser*, which shows Uncle Sam and Winston Churchill busy erecting gravestones to ships which the Japanese claimed, often erroneously, their forces had sunk

'The Boomerang': Hitler discovers his attack on Kerch has not quite worked out the way he anticipated – by Canadian cartoonist John Collins

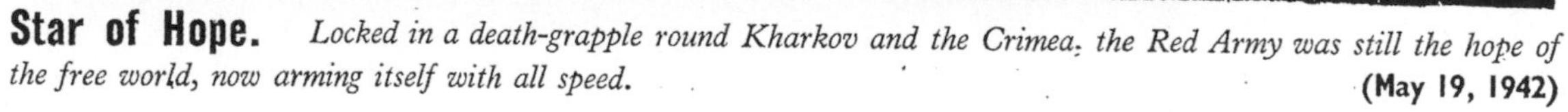
Star of Hope. *Locked in a death-grapple round Kharkov and the Crimea, the Red Army was still the hope of the free world, now arming itself with all speed.* **(May 19, 1942)**

It might be hard to imagine now, but the Red Army briefly became a beacon of hope for the West, as shown in Philip Zec's *Daily Mirror* offering

Despite the sacrifice of hundreds of thousands of troops, Hitler still couldn't find the key to taking Stalingrad. This is how Zec saw the turning point in the war

'Churchill's New Year's Day Hangover' (*Katzenjammer* means 'the wailing of cats' and 'hangover' in German): rancid drunken alleycats crawl all over Winston Churchill who is in a terrible state after consuming his home-made punch made from lies and illusions (passing reference is also made on cats' collars to the recent loss of HMS *Repulse* and the *Prince of Wales*, sunk by Japanese aircraft in the Far East)

Above: group portrait of the leaders of the Axis powers drawn by the talented Walter Trier, a German-speaking Jew from Prague who produced leaflets for the Ministry of Information after fleeing Germany in 1936. Later, he emigrated to Canada; right: 'Hitler at Stalingrad' – Kukryniksy imagine Hitler's face in the mirror after defeat in the 'city of steel'

Walter Trier neatly encapsulated the story of what happened when Adolf met Josef

Suddenly, it seemed, everybody was lining up to take a swing at Hitler. This British poster for part-time war workers drew on the new mood of optimism

Desert Song. *It was the End of the Beginning. British and American troops landed in Algeria, and, with Montgomery's Eighth Army, began to squeeze the Axis out of the Mediterranean.* **(November 9, 1942)**

After the Torch Landings in November 1942 which saw American troops disembarking on the Vichy French shores of North Africa, Axis hopes in the region were clearly doomed. Here Philip Zec portrays the despair of German Field Marshal Erwin Rommel, and French politicians Philippe Petain (with moustache) and Pierrre Laval (in dark suit)

'This is the Enemy': a classic US poster that was translated into many languages, including Italian (as seen here) – it was painted by Karl Koehler and Victor Ancona

HOJA POPULAR No. 2 — Edición de: ARTISTAS LIBRES DE MEXICO — FEBRERO 22 DE 1942

BUENA ES LA LIBERTAD, PERO...

El pueblo nunca puede emparejarse, con esto de las rentas altas y los bajos salarios.

Resulta que la mejor parte de las ganancias de la gente que trabaja se va en pagar la casa.

¡Y qué casas! Las mismas vecindades del tiempo de Don Porfirio, sucias, destartaladas, apestosas, amontonando en el menor espacio posible el mayor número posible de inquilinos. Son como vacas lecheras que siguen poduciendo a través de los años, llueva o truene, bajo el aguijón del cobrador. Y algo semejante pasa ya con las modernas casas de departamentos, que por el tamaño de las piezas más parecen anaqueles de botica. "Esta es la salita..." le dicen a uno, y son dos metros cuadrados en el vano de una escalera. "Este es el bañito..." ¡y no cabe ni el gato! En cuanto al sol, el aire y la luz, son lujos de ricos.

Las composturas que se hacen necesarias en las vecindades-chiqueros y en los departamentos para enanos, tardan más en llegar a la tierra que la luz de una estrella lejana; pero en cambio ¡qué rápida, qué puntual, qué infalible es siempre la llegada del recibo!

Buena culpa de la situación difícil del pueblo trabajador la tienen las rentas altas. Cada peso que se paga de más por la vivienda significa menos comida, menos ropa, menos medicinas, menos instrucción para los hijos...

Esto no quita que, SI LOS DEJAMOS, los pobrecitos dueños de casas suban otro poco las rentas EN VISTA DE LA GUERRA. ¡Dos pesos más en Peralvillo por la toma de Singapur! ¡Quince pesos más en Bolívar por la próxima caída de Smolensk! Pues los propietarios, como los tenderos, siempre están muy bien enterados de lo que pasa en el mundo.

Al fin y al cabo habrá que "arrendarlos" en corto, pues como dijo el otro, "BUENA ES LA LIBERTAD, PERO NO ENSUCIAR EL GORRO"...

SUELDOS BAJOS
HABITACIONES CHICAS
RENTAS GRANDES

No le ajusta... el tacuchito

Dijo el indito: Nones... Pancha

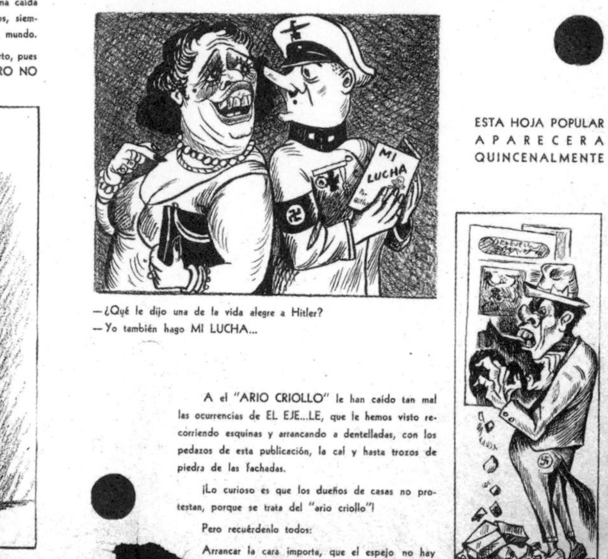

—¿Qué le dijo una de la vida alegre a Hitler?
—Yo también hago MI LUCHA...

ESTA HOJA POPULAR APARECERA QUINCENALMENTE

A el "ARIO CRIOLLO" le han caído tan mal las ocurrencias de EL EJE...LE, que le hemos visto recorriendo esquinas y arrancando a dentelladas, con los pedazos de esta publicación, la cal y hasta trozos de piedra de las fachadas.

¡Lo curioso es que los dueños de casas no protestan, porque se trata del "ario criollo"!

Pero recuérdenlo todos:

Arrancar la cara importa, que el espejo no hay que.

Above: an anti-fascist broadside from the Mexican magazine, *El Eje. .Le*, with a cover which cocks a snook at Hitler, then shows Franco in bed with Hitler and, below that, the couple are canoodling over a copy of *Mein Kampf*

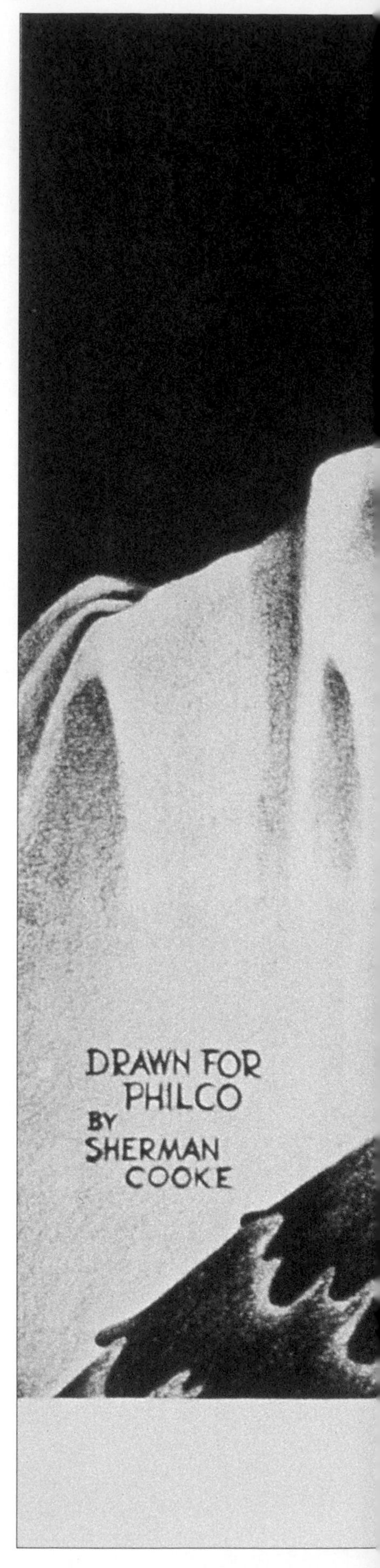

Right: US poster by Sherman Cooke

Time is Short, Adolph!

WAITING THEIR HOUR

[On December 17th, 1939, the first contingent of the Canadian Army, now in Britain, landed on our shores.]

E.H. Shepard's celebration of Canada's contribution to the Allied war effort – without friends like this, events might have gone quite differently for Britain and the rest of the free world

Johnny Canuck was a lumberjack when he first turned up as the embodiment of Canada in 1869. He was reinvented as an action hero by cartoonist Leo Bachle for Bell's "*Dime*" *Comics* in February 1941, and went on to win the war virtually single-handed after a brief encounter wtih Adolf Hitler

"They won't let on who the camp is for."

Frank Hoar was a British architect who designed the original terminal for Gatwick airport. He also worked under the name 'Acanthus' for such magazines as *Punch* and *The New Yorker*

"Shall we join the ladies?"

Acanthus produced many cartoons about the 'Home Front' during the war and this one is a classic of its type

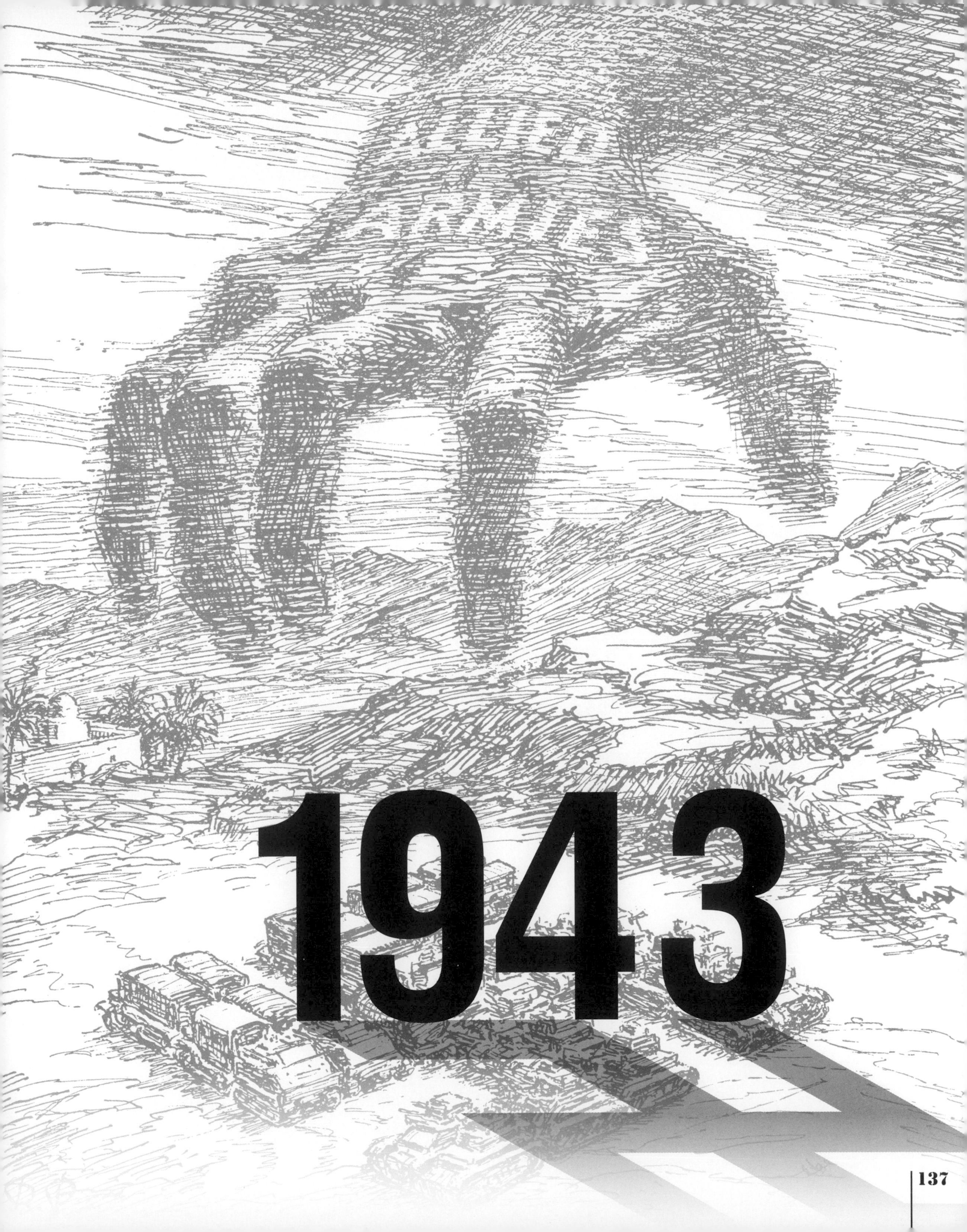

1943

THE FATES DECIDE.

E.H. Shepard illustrated *Winnie the Pooh* and *The Wind in the Willows*, and also drew the Big Cuts (full-page political cartoons) for *Punch* magazine. In 1945 he succeeded Bernard Partridge as *Punch*'s senior cartoonist, but he felt he wasn't particulary well suited to the role since he had no particular interest in politics. He also used to agonize over whether he had achieved a good likeness of the characters he was drawing. Shepard served in World War I and won the Military Cross at Ypres in 1917. 'The Fates Decide' is one of his masterpieces

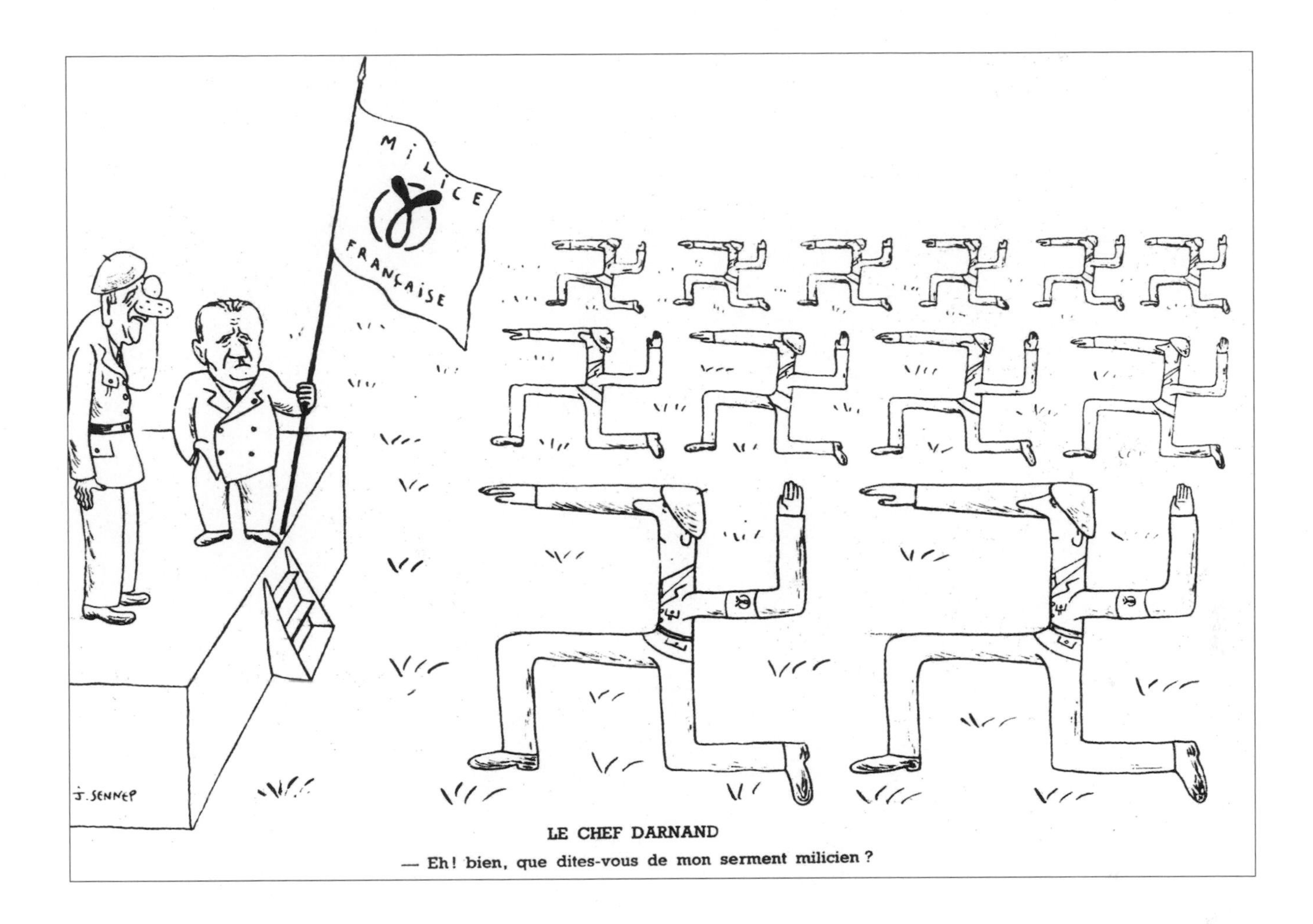

Joseph Darnand, leader of the Vichy French collaborators, is saying, 'What do you think of the *milice*'s oath of loyalty?' [*milice* means militia] – by Sennep

ЧЕГО ГИТЛЕР ХОЧЕТ
земля помещикам!
1. ХОЧЕТ–ХЛЕБ У КРЕСТЬЯН ОТНЯТЬ
2. ХОЧЕТ–ЗАВОДЫ БУРЖУЯМ ОТДАТЬ
3. ХОЧЕТ–ЗЕМЛЮ УСЕЯТЬ ГРОБАМИ
4. ХОЧЕТ–СВОБОДНЫХ СДЕЛАТЬ РАБАМИ
И ЧТО ОН ПОЛУЧИТ
ПОЛУЧИТ–ВТРОЕ ЗА КАЖДЫЙ УДАР
ДЕСЯТКИ ПОЖАРОВ ЗА КАЖДЫЙ ПОЖАР
ПОЛУЧИТ–ШТЫК, ОГОНЬ И СВИНЕЦ
ПОЛУЧИТ–ФАШИЗМА БЕССЛАВНЫЙ КОНЕЦ

Left: 'What Hitler wants and what he'll get' by Mikhail Cheremnykh, co-founder of satirical magazine *Krokodil* – this poster is from 1941, but by 1943 its prediction had proved uncannily accurate; above: 'I started up like this but ended up this way' – Kukryniksy allowed themselves a little schadenfreude following Hitler's defeat in Russia

МИФ
О НЕПОБЕДИМОСТИ
ГЕРМАНСКОЙ
АРМИИ
Бор. Ефимов

Left: 'Jerry in Winter': Hitler and Goebbels sadly survey their battered army in retreat – by Boris Yefimov; above: 'Transformation of the Krauts' by Kukryniksy tells its own story about the high cost of invading Mother Russia

Above: Churchill heads a phalanx of British men who mean business – by David Low; left: mounted on a skeletal horse, Hitler takes the lonely road home like Napoleon before him – by Daniel Fitzpatrick; right: 'I Have Lost the Ring': a bedraggled, moany Hitler laments the loss of his ring at Stalingrad (and the 22 divisions within it) – by Kukryniksy

"We have taken up new positions on the Eastern Wall."

Nazi Radio.

Hurled back from Stalingrad, German troops could only wait as the Red Army prepared for its final drive.

(January 27, 1943)

"Blimey! 'E ain't arf getting a ticking-off!"

The First and Eighth Armies linked up in Tunisia for the final drive in Africa.

(March 3, 1943)

Above left: Philip Zec drew a Russian bear that looked uncannily like Stalin with Hitler's head mounted on the wall behind; left: the tide had turned and Zec now viewed defeating the Germans in North Africa as a mopping-up operation; above: Roosevelt puts the New Deal out to pasture, while he gets on with winning the war – by Pulitzer Prize winning artist Clifford Berryman

CLOSING ON TUNIS

Now it was the swastika that looked vulnerable, as illustrated by Bernard Partridge in *Punch* magazine. *Punch* had its paper ration increased because the British government viewed it as a vital contributor to the war effort

Field Marshal Montgomery, *aka* Monty, became the hero of the hour as the Eighth Army swept all before it – by Philip Zec in the *Daily Mirror*

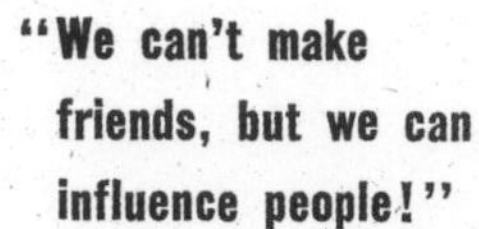
"We can't make friends, but we can influence people!"

As the Axis began to crack, the Gestapo stepped-up its drive to keep enslaved Europe in chains.

(March 16, 1943)

Above: Goebbels' words rang hollow as more and more German atrocities came to light – by Philip Zec in the *Daily Mirror*; left: 'DIGGER Home on Leave: "Now don't forget you're only a mascot."' An Australian soldier provides some last-minute instructions to his lady friend as he waits for his wife to answer the door – by Joan Morrison; opposite: a warning to Germans to observe the black-out – 'The Enemy Can See Your Light'!

Der Feind sieht Dein Licht!
Verdunkeln!
DPA
Sander Herweg

Marry in haste . . .
repent at leisure.

With the Allies in Sicily, and his country weary of a lost war, the Duce, for want of a better home, resigned and fled to the uneasy bosom of his Fuehrer.

(July 23, 1943)

Above: the SS attempted to rescue Mussolini when he was imprisoned by the Italian government, as seen at the time by Philip Zec; right: a Russian soldier's drawing of 'Fritz in the Cold'

The insect crawls out of the stone.

The Beginning of the End came, and Himmler, uneasy about German morale, now turned his whip on his own people.

(August 24, 1943)

Above: in the *Daily Mirror* Philip Zec satirised Himmler's attempts to lift German morale. Strength Through Joy was the official German tourist agency that had encouraged German workers to become fit by promoting active holiday activities such as skiing and hiking

"I've been drafted to combined operations, Sir—am I at the right place?"

Suddenly everyone was pooling resources to send the Germans back where they came from – this amusing image was by Anton. ('Anton' was the brother and sister combination of Harold and Beryl Yeoman)

The man who re-planned Berlin.

The Architect of War saw his plans go up in flame as the Allied Air Forces came to Germany.

(November 26. 1943)

This cartoon by Philip Zec was inspired by the famous Hitler quote of 1939: 'I am at heart a simple architect.' In 1908 Hitler had hoped to study architecture at the Vienna Academy, but his family was too poor to afford the tuition fees so he never achieved his teenage ambition

"HE USED TO BE A PURSUIT PILOT."

Above: *G.I. Joe* was the creation of serving soldier Sgt. Dave Breger and his strip led to the widespread usage of the term in wartime; opposite above: *The Sad Sack*, a term which might translate as 'loser' today, was invented by Sgt. George Baker and syndicated after 1945; left and right: these individual cartoons were drawn by US servicemen during the war

"AIN'T BEEN IN LONG, HAVE YOU, MATE?"

—Leo Salkin, PhoM3c, USN, San Diego, Cal.

1944

LIBERATORS
MISS AMERICA
KU-KLUX-K
MISS VICTOR
$
JITTERBUG - Triumph of Civilisation
WORLD'S
MOST BEAUTIFUL LEGS
De U.S.A. zullen de Europeesche Kultuur van den ondergang redden
8/7 – 8/8 '44
LEEST STORM-SS.

Labour organisation in the Škoda armament factories.

Left: this SS poster by Leest Storm shows the USA as a monster destroying European culture underfoot and rampaging through the Netherlands in the guise of liberator; above: a cartoon by Stephen shows the situation in the armaments factories in Czechoslovakia, several of which produced top secret weapons for the occupying Germans; right: 'Fascist Crow, we don't have any lambs here [*in Russia*]' by Soviet artist Viktor Deni

Philip Zec cartoon with Winston Churchill performing his 'On your marks' routine by the White Cliffs of Dover

US poster exhorting the public to buy more war bonds on the pretext of helping Japanese Emperor Hirohito to fund his own suicide kit

Bill Mauldin

Bill Mauldin was born in New Mexico in 1921 and enlisted in the US army in 1940 after serving in the Arizona Guard.

As a sergeant with the 45th Division, Mauldin landed in Sicily and worked as a cartoonist for *Stars & Stripes* as well as the company magazine. He was given his own personal jeep to drive around in and produced around six cartoons a week, providing a warts-and-all version of what life was like for regular US soldiers, known as 'dogfaces', on the front line in Europe and elsewhere. His work was distributed throughout the US army at home and abroad and it was phenomenally popular among serving men.

Mauldin's most famous creations were Willie and Joe, two dirty, unshaven GIs (opposite) who constantly cast doubts over the leadership qualities of their officers and whose laconic utterances left the reader in no doubt that war was a very hard slog indeed – so terrible you had to laugh.

Mauldin's attitude earned him a lengthy lecture from General George Patton who 'threatened to throw his ass in jail for spreading dissent', but Dwight Eisenhower defended the cartoonist on the grounds that his work provided a safety valve for the frustrations of GIs.

Mauldin was wounded by a mortar shell near Monte Cassino in 1943. He decided to have Willie and Joe killed off on the very last day of combat, but the staff at *Stars & Stripes* dissuaded him from doing the deed. He won the Pulitzer Prize in 1945.

"I got a hangover. Does it show?"

F.D. Roosevelt won the 1944 US election, routing opponents such as Yellow Press baron William Randolph Hearst, Tom Dewey and J. Edgar Hoover – by radical US cartoonist Ben Yomen, this image was syndicated worldwide

"Well, if they don't come in three minutes, they'll just 'ave to storm the defences."

Rowland Emett was a builder of whimsical kinetic sculptures whose cartoons were regularly published in *Punch* magazine

Ex-advertising illustrator William Garnet 'Bing' Coughlin served with Canada's 4th Princess Louise Dragoon Guards (*aka* 'The Plugs' or 'Piddly-Gees') during WWII and fought in the Italian campaign. Like Bill Mauldin, his work spoke up for the enlisted man against the officer class which led to its immense popularity during the war years. Herbie (above) was Coughlin's answer to Mauldin's Willie and Joe. Regular soldiers in the Canadian army became known as 'Herbies' after this singularly heroic chinless fighting man

'What's Cookin'?': Australian artist Noel Counihan pictured a frustrated Hitler astride a bomb which is about to go off. The situation seems to imply that Hitler lit the fuse himself

"They say, can we do two hundred and eighty-seven Dainty Afternoon Teas?"

Rowland Emett liked to produce cheerful cartoons of a familiar everyday England even though the country was at war

"Here's another complaint about low-flying from the local Archery Club."

Similarly, Acanthus kept the jokes coming as wartime England began at last to see the light at the end of the tunnel

There is no weak link.

The end approached. Hitler launched his flying-bombs in swarms on battered South-eastern England. But London could still take it.

(July 4, 1944)

61

Above: Hitler's last throw of the dice against Britain after the D-Day landings was to launch the V-1, *aka* the Buzz Bomb or Doodlebug, at the south of England from the French and Dutch coasts; opposite above: V-1s as viewed by the Nazis in *Das Reich*; opposite below: at this point in the war, Allied bombing of German cities was taking an increasing toll, as noted by Philip Zec

". . . and stop whistling 'Night and Day'!"

All the slave-workers that Germany could muster could not stop the round-the-clock bombing offensive which softened-up her war factories.

(March 13, 1944)

The Hour of Reckoning. (June 7, 1944)

Allied forces were on Germany's doorstep and they were not in the mood to knock before entering – by Philip Zec in the *Daily Mirror*

An anti-collaborator cartoon from Holland in mock-Russian Constructivist style shows two scenes side by side: Allied soldiers landing at Arnhem by parachute during their disastrous raid (Operation Market Garden); and a woman dancing on a piano to entertain Nazis. Behind her is the inscription: 'We are the conscience of the nation'

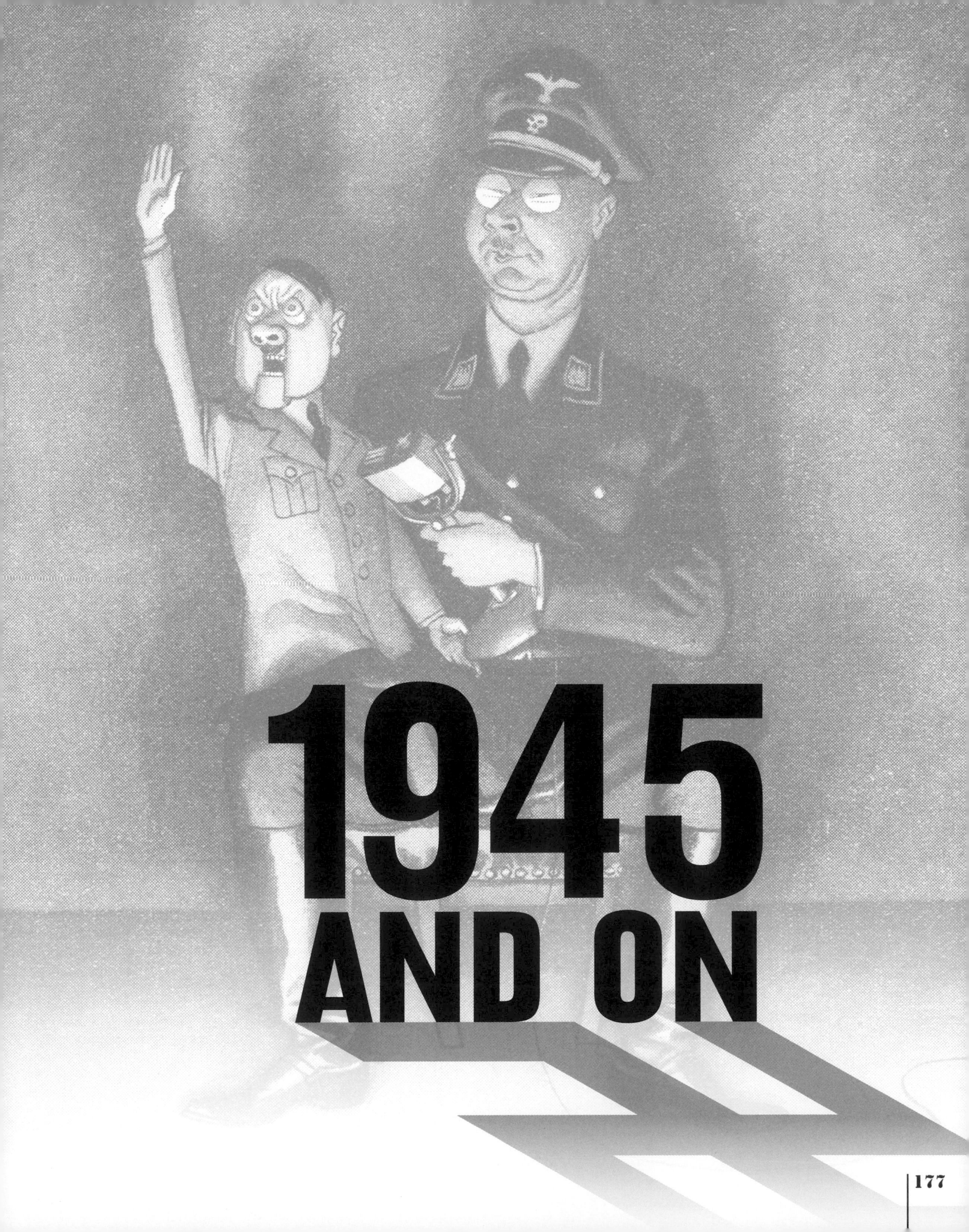

1945 AND ON

A German leaflet cunningly designed to demoralize British troops who might not wish to risk their lives with the end of the war in sight. Accompanying text said: 'Why walk the tightrope between life and death in 1945, become a prisoner of war'

'Reap as You Have Sown!': Viktor Deni's poster was not averse to kicking a man when he was down, not if that man was Adolf Hitler

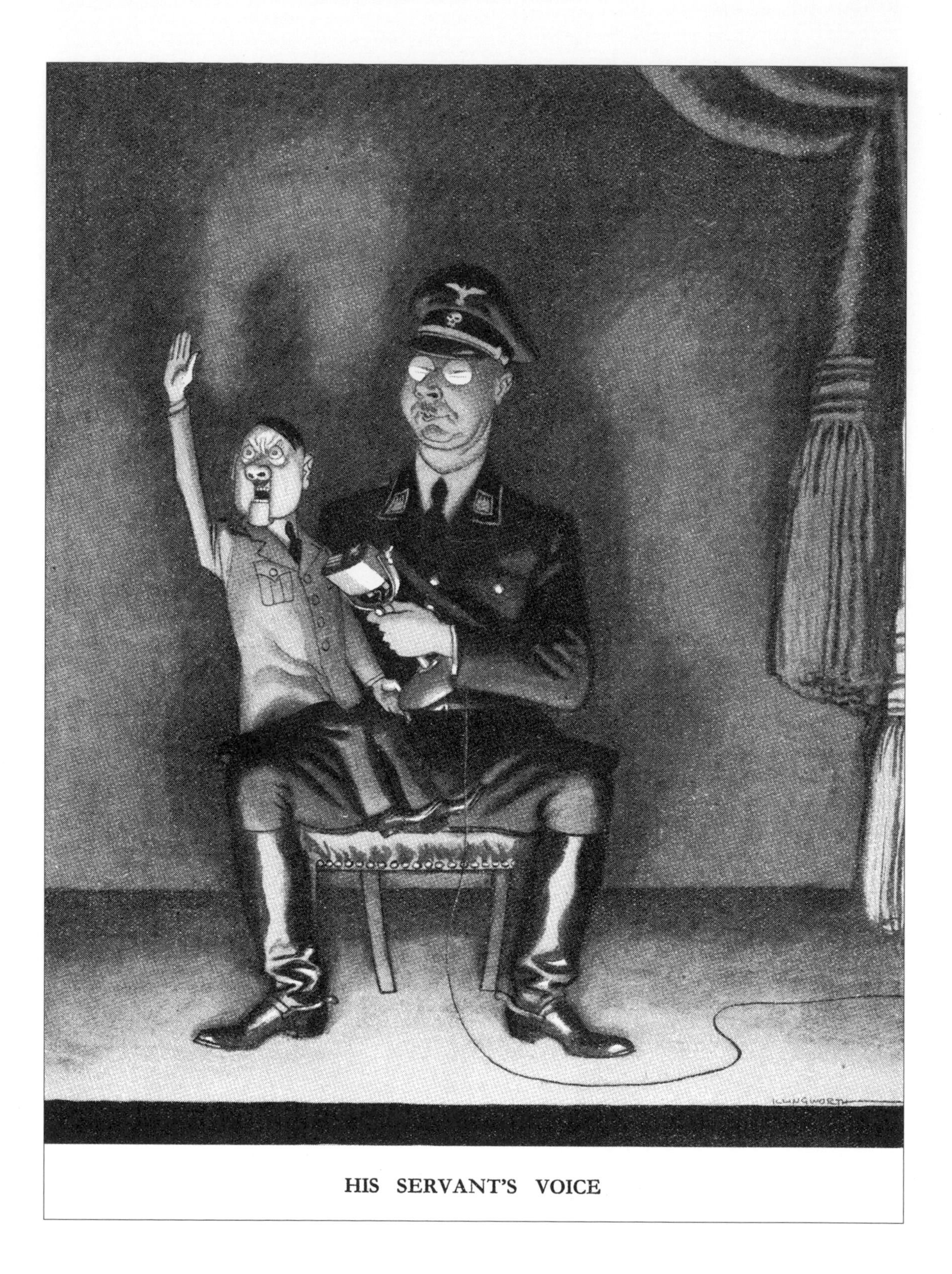

HIS SERVANT'S VOICE

Leslie Illingworth's brilliant drawing of Hitler as Himmler's puppet was designed to reinforce the growing perception that Himmler had taken over the reins in Germany, with Hitler a spent force

British triumphalism led to a new breed of greetings card being churned out for use of those on the front line

"This trick will have to be ruddy marvellous."

As defeat loomed, and up till the last weeks, Hitler still threatened more and more frightful secret weapons. They came too late . . . but only just.

(March 1, 1945)

Goebbels and Himmler look on ratlike and aghast as demented conjuror Adolf Hitler runs out of tricks – by Philip Zec in the *Daily Mirror*

The cover of *Yank* magazine, designed and produced by serving soldiers Sgt. Frank Burke and Private First Class Tom Flannery, shows the Allies as they face up to the necessity of making decisions on the future of Europe

"As far as I'm concerned I don't care if I never see another uniform."

In Britain, returning soldiers stepped out of army uniforms into the familiar garb of Civvy Street. Every man was issued with a 'demob suit' that was virtually identical to the suit given to everyone else. The suits were made en masse by the tailoring company Burton and were renowned for being hard-wearing but ill-fitting…

Old hand Frank Reynolds produced cartoons for *Punch* in World War I and continued to do so throughout WWII

A series of vignettes of life in the New Zealand Expeditionary Forces in Egypt and Italy during World War II – by Neville Colvin. Colvin was a cartoonist with the *Wellington Evening Post*. He moved to London after the war and drew the *Modesty Blaise* strip from 1980 to 1986

"Thank you for light in the darkest hours." *Britain showed by an overwhelming Labour vote that it had had enough of Tory rule. But Churchill's personal war leadership will never be forgotten.* **(August 16, 1945)**

Philip Zec's tribute to Winston Churchill in the *Daily Mirror* after Britain's great wartime leader lost the 1945 general election to Clement Attlee and the Labour Party

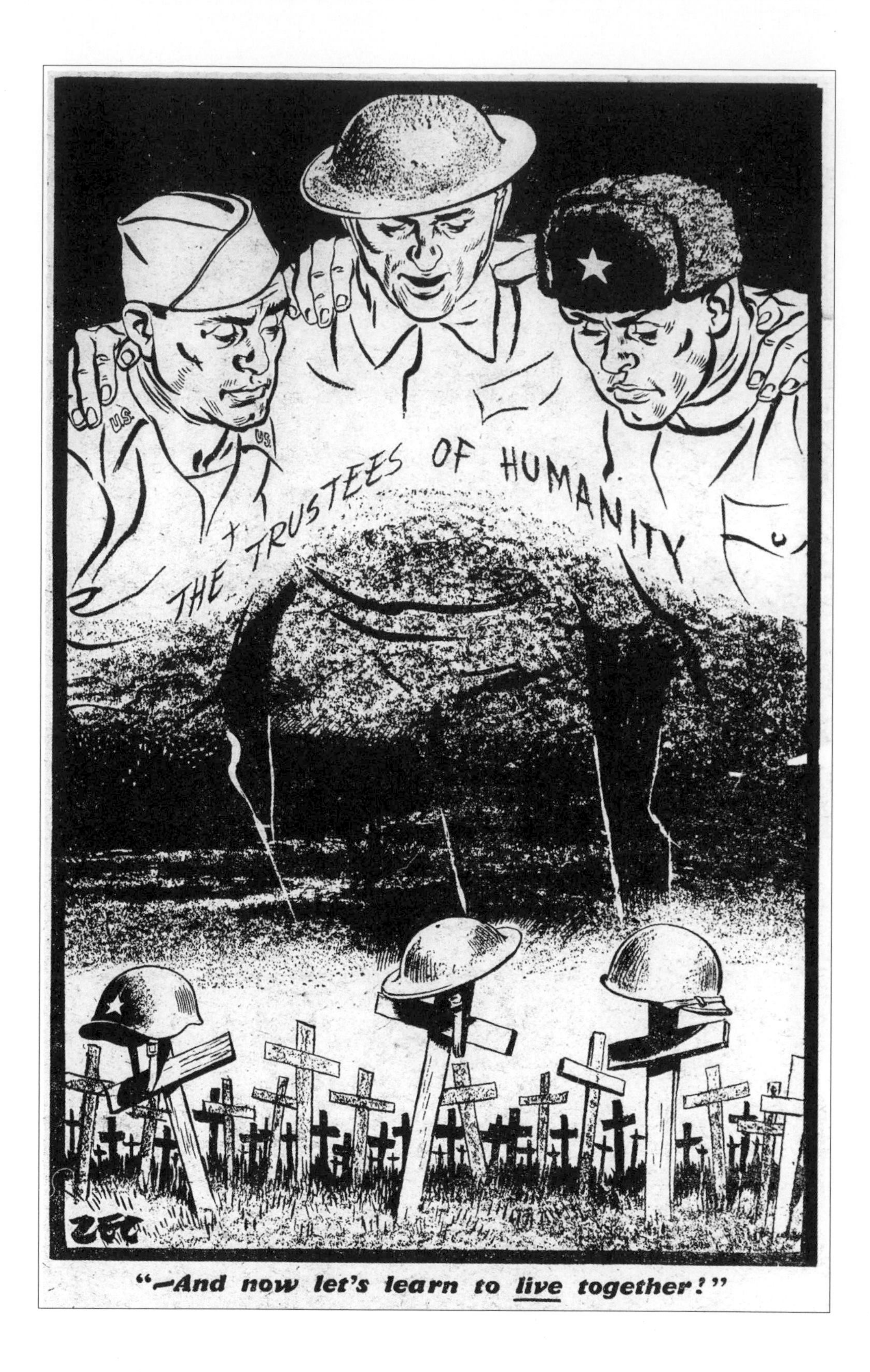

The end of the war marked the beginning of a period of idealism with people united in their determination to forge a better future - by Philip Zec in the *Daily Mirror*

"Here you are! Don't lose it again!"

Philip Zec repeats his message of hope

'End of the Road': in the US Daniel Fitzpatrick offered cold comfort for those who were up before the judges at Nuremberg

'The Last Figure': a courtoom sketch by Kukryniksy from the Nuremberg Trials: the most important criminal hearings ever held, they established the principle that criminals will always be held responsible for their actions under international law. This brought closure to World War II, allowing the reconstruction process to begin

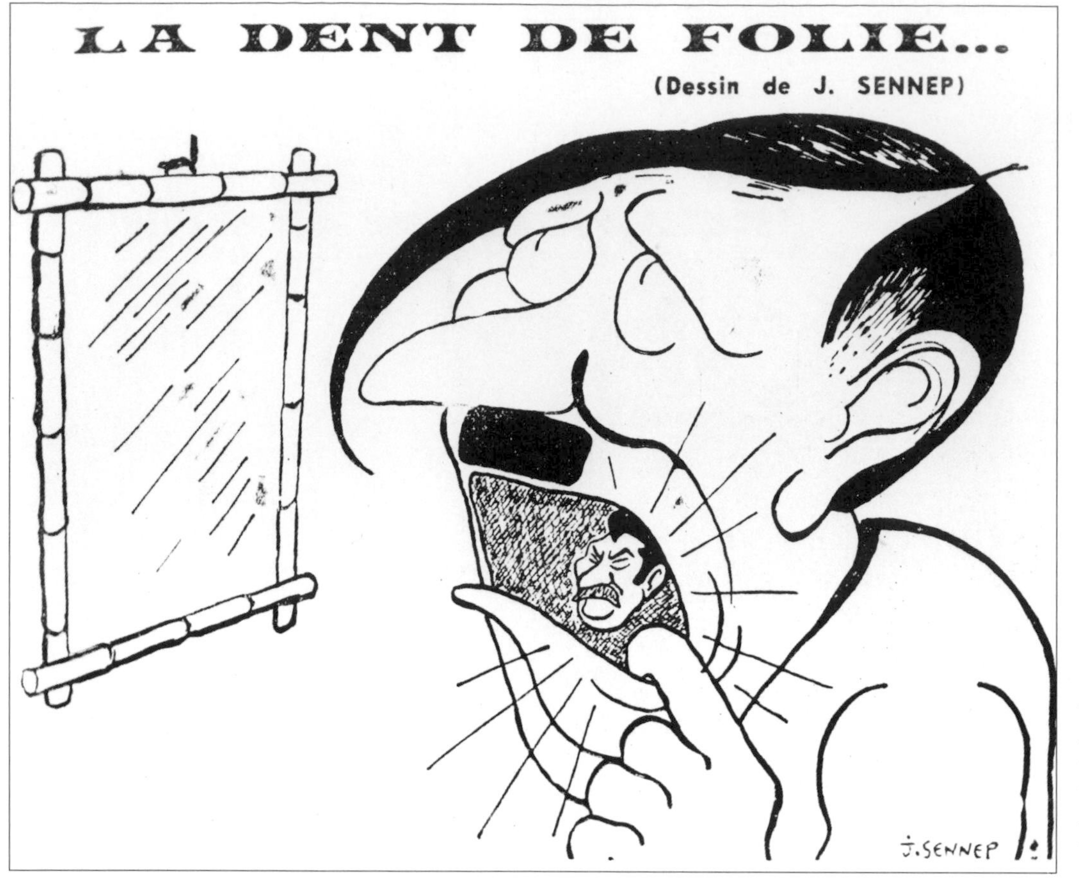

'Maddening Toothache': Adolf Hitler discovers the source of the pain – by Sennep, 1939-40

PICTURE CREDITS

We have made every effort to contact the copyright holders of the images used in this book. In a few cases, we have been unable to do so, but we will be very happy to credit them in future editions.

Alamy: 14 (Photos 12), 18 (World History Archive), 19 (Mary Evans Picture Library), 21 (Photos 12), 22b (Photos 12), 24 (INTERFOTO), 27 (Photos 12), 28 (Mary Evans Picture Library), 29 (Photos 12), 45, 48 (Pictorial Press Ltd), 52b (INTERFOTO), 62t and 62b (INTERFOTO), 65 (Photos 12), 68b (Photos 12), 78 (World History Archive), 79 (Photos 12), 92 (The Art Gallery Collection), 101 (Mary Evans Picture Library, 117b (Mary Evans Picture Library), 120 (moss), 125b (Mary Evans Picture Library), 127 (Pictorial Press Ltd), 130 (World History Archive), 139 (Photos 12), 145, 152b, 165t

Alexander Turnbull Library, Wellington, New Zealand: 44, 86, 186

Atlas Van Stolk, Rotterdam: 71, 88

Australian War Memorial: 150b, 169

The Bridgeman Art Library: 72 (Archives Charmet), 131, 183

Corbis: 10-11 (Bettmann), 95

ED Archives: 181t, 181b

Getty Images: 63 (Popperfoto), 102, 115, 144t, 147, 160, 163, 166, 178

Library and Archives Canada: 133, 168t, 168b

Mary Evans Picture Library: 49, 82 (Illustrated London News Ltd), 100, 175 (Onslow Auctions Ltd)

McCord Museum, Canada: 121 (M965.199.3456)

Mirrorpix: 52t, 94, 122, 123, 128, 146t, 146b, 149, 150t, 152t, 153, 155, 172, 173b, 174, 182, 187, 188, 189

Ohio State University Library Special Collection: 37

Reproduced with permission of Punch Limited (www.punch.co.uk): 8, 9, 26, 30, 32, 33, 34, 35, 38t, 42, 43, 46, 54, 55, 58, 59, 66–67, 73, 80, 81, 83, 84, 85, 108, 109, 110, 111, 116, 132, 134, 135, 138, 148, 154, 167, 170, 171, 180, 184, 185

RIA NOVOSTI: 6, 22t, 93, 96, 97, 114, 140, 141, 142, 143, 161b, 179, 191

State Historical Society of Missouri: 69, 70, 190

TopFoto: 16, 20 (The Granger Collection), 23 (ullsteinbild), 25, 31 (Artmedia/HIP), 47, 64 (The National Archives/Heritage-Images), 89t (The Granger Collection), 103 (Topham Picturepoint), 104 (The Granger Collection), 105 (World History Archive), 106, 107, 125t (Topham Picturepoint), 144b (The Granger Collection), 162

US Library of Congress: 192